KNOWLEDGE-BASED SYSTEMS:
Implications
for Human—Computer Interfaces

ELLIS HORWOOD BOOKS IN INFORMATION TECHNOLOGY
General Editor: Dr. JOHN M. M. PINKERTON, Principal, McLean Pinkerton Associates, Surrey, (formerly Manager of Strategic Requirements, ICL)

EXPERT SYSTEMS IN BUSINESS: A Practical Approach
M. BARRETT, Expertech Limited, Slough, and A. BEEREL, Lysia Limited, London
ELECTRONIC DATA PROCESSING, Vols. 1 and 2*
M. BECKER, R. HABERFELLNER and G. LIEBETRAU, Zurich, Switzerland
EXPERT SYSTEMS: Strategic Implications and Applications
A. BEEREL, Lysia Limited, London
SOFTWARE ENGINEERING ENVIRONMENTS
P. BRERETON, Department of Computer Science, University of Keele
SMART CARDS: Their Principles, Practice and Applications*
R. BRIGHT, Information Technology Strategies International Limited, Orpington, Kent
PRACTICAL MACHINE TRANSLATION*
D. CLARKE and U. MAGNUSSON-MURRAY, Department of Applied Computing and Mathematics, Cranfield Institute of Technology, Bedford
KNOWLEDGE-BASED SYSTEMS: Implications for Human–Computer Interfaces
D. CLEAL, PA Computers and Telecommunications, London, and N. HEATON, Central Computer and Telecommunications Agency, London
KNOWLEDGE-BASED MANAGEMENT SUPPORT SYSTEMS*
G. I. DOUKIDIS, F. LAND and G. MILLER, Information Management Department, London Business School
KNOWLEDGE ELICITATION*
M. GREENWELL, Expert Systems International, Oxford
KNOWLEDGE-BASED EXPERT SYSTEMS IN INDUSTRY
J. KRIZ, Head of AI Group, Brown Boveri Research Systems, Switzerland
ARTIFICIAL INTELLIGENCE: Current applications*
A. MATTHEWS and J. RODDY, Aregon International Ltd., London
INFORMATION TECHNOLOGY: An Overview*
J. M. M. PINKERTON, McLean Pinkerton Associates, Esher, Surrey
EXPERT SYSTEMS IN THE ORGANISATION: An Introduction for Decision-Makers*
S. SAVORY, Nixdorf Computers AG, FRG
BUILDING EXPERT SYSTEMS: Cognitive Emulation
P. E. SLATTER, Product Designer, Telecomputing plc, Oxford
SPEECH AND LANGUAGE-BASED COMMUNICATION WITH MACHINES:
Towards the Conversational Computer*
J. A. WATERWORTH and M. TALBOT, Human Factors Division, British Telecom Research Laboratories, Ipswich

* In preparation

KNOWLEDGE-BASED SYSTEMS:
Implications for Human–Computer Interfaces

D. M. CLEAL
Consultant, PA Computers and Telecommunications, London
and
N. O. HEATON
HUSAT Research Centre, Department of Human Sciences
Loughborough University of Technology

ELLIS HORWOOD LIMITED
Publishers · Chichester

Halsted Press: a division of
JOHN WILEY & SONS
New York · Chichester · Brisbane · Toronto

First published in 1988 by
ELLIS HORWOOD LIMITED
Market Cross House, Cooper Street,
Chichester, West Sussex, PO19 1EB, England
*The publisher's colophon is reproduced from James Gillison's drawing of the ancient
Market Cross, Chichester.*

Distributors:

Australia and New Zealand:
JACARANDA WILEY LIMITED
GPO Box 859, Brisbane, Queensland 4001, Australia

Canada:
JOHN WILEY & SONS CANADA LIMITED
22 Worcester Road, Rexdale, Ontario, Canada

Europe and Africa:
JOHN WILEY & SONS LIMITED
Baffins Lane, Chichester, West Sussex, England

North and South America and the rest of the world:
Halsted Press: a division of
JOHN WILEY & SONS
605 Third Avenue, New York, NY 10158, USA

South-East Asia
JOHN WILEY & SONS (SEA) PTE LIMITED
37 Jalan Pemimpin # 05–04
Block B, Union Industrial Building, Singapore 2057

Indian Subcontinent
WILEY EASTERN LIMITED
4835/24 Ansari Road
Daryaganj, New Delhi 110002, India

© **1988 D.M. Cleal and N.O. Heaton/Ellis Horwood Limited**

British Library Cataloguing in Publication Data
Cleal, D. M. (David Murray), *1961–*
Knowledge based systems: Implications for human–computer interfaces. —
(Ellis Horwood series in expert systems).
1. Expert systems
I. Title   II. Heaton, N. O. (Nigel O.)
006.3'3
Library of Congress CIP Data available

ISBN 0–7458–0152–8 (Ellis Horwood Limited)
ISBN 0–470–21082–6 (Halsted Press)

Printed in Great Britain by Unwin Bros. of Woking

Contents

Preface

Ever since the construction of the world's first general-purpose computer, many researchers have worked towards the day when machines might possess intelligence comparable with that of humans. At the same time, others have been concerned with ensuring that the existing computer systems can be used to best advantage by people other than their builders. Very roughly, these two areas of research can be described as artificial intelligence and human factors.

Expert systems represent the most exciting fruit of artificial intelligence research to date. Such systems are starting to be employed in everyday life, and these applications rank amongst the most complex computer systems ever built; never before has the expertise of the human factors specialist in making such systems comprehensible been more vital. At the same time, the application of techniques developed by artificial intelligence specialists are proving to be of crucial value in addressing many of the problems that have been identified by the human factors research community.

The book grew out of experience of a number of projects, which the authors, whose backgrounds are in the two main fields described, were involved with. These raised many areas where the experience of one is relevant to the problems of the other, and this book attempts to describe some of this overlap between the two fields, and some of the exciting potential for better systems which can arise out of this synergy. To this end, a number of examples have been drawn together to illustrate the overall theme; that the human factors specialists need their artificial intelligence counterparts, and vice versa.

Most of the areas covered in this book are still the subject of active research. In many cases we have been unable to do much more than describe guiding principles, and point the interested reader in the direction of more detailed sources of information. The objective of this book is to serve not as a detailed manual, but rather an introduction to the potential power of some key developments to enhance the usability and worth of a vast array of computer-based tools.

The book is aimed at people with an active interest in IT, including managers, technical specialists and students. It covers commercial developments, as well as academic research, and should be read by everybody concerned with these rapidly changing fields.

1

Introduction

'Computers are machines and machines exist for one purpose and that purpose is to serve people'

Prof. Alphonse Chapanis

1.1 INTRODUCTION

Recent years have seen a trend towards the development of ever more complex computer systems. This trend seems unlikely to be reversed: intelligent knowledge-based systems (IKBSs), currently hailed as the future of modern computing, are undoubtedly among the most complex computer programs ever written.

This deepening complexity has not always been matched by an equal level of concern for the user, who must come to terms with these complex systems. For example, as recently as 1980 the US Navy scrapped an unusable computer at a cost of $30 million with the observation that 'technology-drunk technicians may be buying weapons too complex for actual use'.

This example highlights a major problem with recent developments at the frontiers of computing: as machines become more complex, there arises a very real danger that they will prove too complicated for users to gain full benefit from their application.

The beginnings of the widespread use of knowledge-based systems, and in particular expert systems, brought the matter to a head. When a computer system is similar in complexity to a human expert (in terms of its approach to certain well-defined tasks in a given domain) it becomes necessary to allow for a level of communication similar to that between human expert and human client. Fortunately, IKBS techniques bring not only the problem, but also the potential to solve it.

Thus the primary thrust of this book is to consider ways in which IKBS techniques can be harnessed to enable the relationship between humans and their ever more sophisticated computer tools to develop as effectively as possible. Two themes are central to our view of this developing partnership, and their presence will be detected running throughout this book.

1.2 MAJOR THEMES

The first theme is the growing importance of user-centred design. It is essential to realise that the adoption of a user-centred approach is more than just a gimmick. The 'user-friendly system' all too often represents little more than standard advertising copy. However, systems which are genuinely easy to use are already more successful. They sell more and produce better results, more accurately and faster than systems which have similar capabilities but worse interfaces.

Until relatively recently, interface design has been about the provision of good hardware, mixing menus and command languages and providing usable help and error messages when and where necessary.

The widespread use of computers by non-programmers and occasional users has caused many developers to review their design philosophy. Unfortunately, in many cases computer systems have been limited by the nature of the hardware and software underlying them.

Our second major theme concerns the development of knowledge-based techniques for system development. Specifically, we consider how these developments influence, and should be influenced by, parallel developments in the study of human-computer interaction.

The recent advances in knowledge-based techniques have struck at the heart of conventional systems design. Programs need no longer follow set procedures based upon fixed control structures. The development of declarative programming languages has led to the design of systems based upon real world knowledge and expertise. We are beginning to reach a clearer understanding of the possibilities of these new systems. Intelligent aids to experts, capable of adapting to new knowledge, are being built. Systems which capture expertise, not only in a precise and unchanging form, but in an adaptable and perhaps vague form, are becoming commercial products.

Thus, to summarise, the needs of human-computer interaction and the potential of knowledge-based programming techniques are beginning to converge. This is caused by

- the design of systems more sophisticated than ever before, yet intended for use by computer-illiterate users

- the development of high quality interfaces which assumes paramount importance.

In expert sysems, the first fruit of artificial intelligence research, we have a set of powerful tools and techniques which enable us, for the first time, to represent that highly complex entity, the user. Knowledge-based techniques enable us to represent aspects of the user's behaviour, capabilities and characteristics which can then be incorporated into the construction of a more interactive interface. Thus, the interaction can be more flexible and adaptable, and therefore more usable.

This capability does cause some problems. It forces the designers to be more insightful and to have a more fundamental understanding of users and their capabilities than before. Similarly, more flexible systems do not, per se, lead to better interaction. There are still many problems which need to be solved.

The aim of this book is to look in detail at the relationship between human factors and knowledge-based systems. We will explore how developments in one area will influence and aid developments in the other. We aim to show that a truly symbiotic relationship between the two disciplines is not only a natural development, but also an essential one. To produce truly useful systems the user must be considered and taken account of. To fully represent the user, the system needs to incorporate something other than conventional techniques.

We will consider many aspects of human factors and knowledge-based programming. Looking at the influence of hardware and software developments on system design, we will see how many systems are designed around the development rather than the user. This is not neccesarily a bad thing, provided the development is good and will provide for a system which might be less limiting and more usable than its predecessors. Ultimately, however, it is still restrictive.

We will consider specific examples of how hardware developments have influenced the design of whole systems, as well as reviewing hardware and its associated HCI (human-computer interaction) considerations - from the keyboard to the speech recogniser.

As has already been mentioned, the influence of psychological models of the user on the design of interfaces is of major importance. We shall look in detail at this influence, and also investigate how such models can be incorporated into the system.

Apart from knowledge-based programming, another area of artificial intelligence research which has recently emerged from the laboratory is the use of computers to interpret and act upon natural language input. We will explore some of the techniques for understanding natural language, and their associated design issues.

Natural language recognition is a special case of the use of artificial intelligence techniques to provide a high quality interface to what may well be a comparatively straightforward underlying system. We shall consider some of the general issues in the design of such systems, and decribe some example systems.

One of the most important features of expert systems is their ability to explain their actions. We will look at the problems of providing explanation facilities in expert systems, and how we can provide genuinely useful explanations, tailored to the particular user's requirements.

We will also present a loose methodology, or set of good practices, for ensuring that human factors considerations are incorporated into the design of an expert system. This methodology is used to maximise ultimate success and to minimise the cost of failure.

To put the ideas and issues raised in this book into perspective we will look at three existing expert systems. By considering the capabilities of these systems and describing their interfaces we will be able to explore the degree to which the user has been considered.

For the system developer, we will present an analysis of the relative merits of different classes of expert system development tools, viewed from a human factors perspective. A table of the most popular products, listing their major features for the interface designer, will be provided.

Firstly, however, we will briefly describe what we mean by 'Human Factors', 'Expert Systems', and some other terminology which recurs in this book. In the remainder of this chapter, we shall consider some of the more wide ranging topics which span several of the specific chapters within this book.

1.3 TERMINOLOGY

Artificial Intelligence is a term used very widely, but one which lacks a precise definition. The original aim of artificial intelligence research was to produce a machine which exhibited intelligence. Even then the definition was vague, because the word 'intelligence' itself is not well defined. Since then, the field has become fragmented, as different researchers have moved in different directions, and thus the term has become less cleary defined.

Nevertheless, the artificial intelligence umbrella is generally held to embrace a range of more specific disciplines, including:

- knowledge-based systems
- machine learning systems
- speech recognition and generation
- robotics

We shall be principally concerned with knowledge-based systems, more commonly described as **Intelligent knowledge-based systems (IKBSs)**. This is also a broad field, encompassing items such as:

- expert systems
- vision systems
- thought support tools
- natural language systems

Within this range of examples, by far and away the most commercial success has been achieved by **expert systems**. Expert systems are unique in another way: whilst the other types of system mentioned may or may not use knowledge-based techniques, expert systems invariably do use those techniques.

There are many definitions of the term **expert system**. One which covers the main points succinctly has been proposed by Max Bramer:

> 'an expert system is a computing system which embodies organised human knowledge concerning some specific area of expertise, sufficient to perform as a skilful and cost-effective consultant.'

This definition describes the expert system from a user viewpoint.

An alternative way of characterising expert systems takes note of their internal architecture. Fig 1.1 shows the familiar general structure of an expert system. The key feature which characterises the expert system architecture is the separation of inference engine and knowledge base. A conventional system will use a separate database to contain data, and a program will access that data. The program contains knowledge about the domain, how to solve problems, the

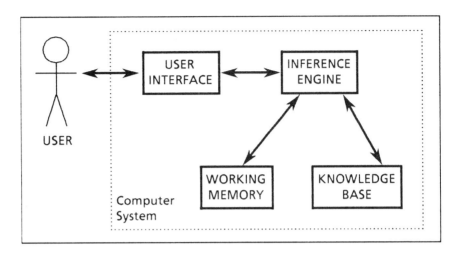

Fig 1.1 Generalised Expert System

structure of the task, and so on. In an expert system, much of that knowledge is separated out from the program and stored explicitly. This knowledge is combined with the data to form a knowledge base

Human Factors or **Ergonomics** is the study of the relationship between the user, the interface, the system and the environment. Often the term **ergonomics** is wrongly understood to refer simply to the study of the hardware and environment. In fact, it is synonymous with the term human factors, although it is more commonly used in Europe than in the USA.

The relationship between human and system from an ergonomic point of view is typified by Shackel's anthropocentric model, shown in fig 1.2. This so-called 'bulls-eye' approach emphasises the need to consider the whole, as well as the parts. It also restates the importance of centering design on the user.

Before entering on the detailed analysis of more specific areas which forms the bulk of the book, it is worthwhile to pause to consider three areas from a broader perspective.

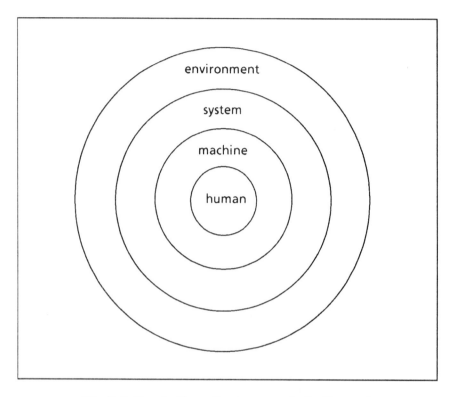

Fig 1.2 Shackel's anthropocentric 'bulls-eye'

1.4 COMPUTER SIMULATION OF THE HUMAN–HUMAN INTERFACE

The first of these three areas is the general issue of computers which, by whatever means, attempt to interact with a human in the way that another human might. Such a computer would, of course, pass the famous 'Turing Test' of machine intelligence. For the reader not familiar with this, the essential idea is that a human interrogates some other entity which is out of sight. Initially, that other entity is a second human. Turing's test then involves that second human being replaced by a computer. The test states that, if the interrogator is unable to detect which is the human and which the computer interviewee, then the computer should be deemed intelligent.

Some early attempts at offering such a level of interaction were surprisingly successful, and yet used very simple

techniques. One of the best examples was Joseph
Weizenbaum's ELIZA (1). This simple, non-directive therapist
surprised many people by the degree of animism which users
were prepared to attribute to the system. It led some people
to claim that the system not only provided much needed
therapy, but was also intelligent. Consider these two
examples, provided by Frudes (2):

' E: Hi, I'm Eliza, what's your problem ?
N: I feel tired
E: Tell me more about such feelings ?
N: I'm not alert
E: Did you come to me because you are not alert ?
N: Yes
E: Are you sure ?
N: Maybe I have other problems too
E: You don't seem quite certain
N: Sorry
E: Please don't apologise

E: Do you often feel sad ?
N: No
E: Are you saying no just to be negative ?
N: Not at all
E: Please don't repeat yourself
N: I'm not
E: Did you come to me because you are not ?
N: Not what ?
E: Why do you ask ?
N: Now I'm really confused
E: How long have you been really confused ?
N: Only since I met you'

Clearly, as far as the user is concerned, the first
conversation might almost pass the 'Turing Test'. Yet a little
more probing, a new line of questioning, and the system is
revealed as merely word-spotting.

In fact, it may be that such programs will have a role to
play in the design of interfaces. Studies by British Telecom's
Research Laboratories as part of the VODIS project (3) on
queries to railway stations show that quite often the

conversation takes the form of repeating the enquirer's question as a statement, perhaps followed by a request for further information. For example:

'E: I want to go to London
S: You want to go to London. When ?'

Such a system would actually require little more intelligence than ELIZA. However, the vagaries of humans are such that other problems emerge. A good case in point is tendency of humans towards non-sequiturs:

'E: I want to go to London
S: You want to go to London. When ?
E: On a train with first class seating and a buffet car.'

The enquirer clearly is not answering the question, but is laying down some conditions which will affect the range of possible responses.

Other studies have approached the issue by looking at interactions between humans, and successively restricting the communications channels between them. Typically, one person is given a plan and a second is given a construction kit. The individual with the plan tells his partner how to assemble the kit. The more modes of communication available, the more efficiently the information is transmitted and the faster the kit is assembled. If the communication is restricted to a teletype, the time taken to transmit the information escalates and the likelihood of success decreases. The importance of this is that it clearly demonstrates that the written word is not sufficient for communicating certain types of information.

Yet this situation is encountered every day by the users of computers. They have complex plans and needs, but are restricted in the way they can communicate. In fact, the situation is even worse than that of the kit assemblers, because the system will not tolerate spelling mistakes, will not attempt to make leaps to understand the overall plan, and so on.

Clearly there is a need to facilitate more 'broad band' communication between user and system. Many other studies have demonstrated the not suprising truth that as more restraints are placed on individuals, so communications deteriorate, more errors occur, and users are less able to express complex ideas.

Thus the importance of novel modes of interaction, even at the lowest level in the dialogue, is demonstrated. We shall be considering many of these in this book, including graphics, natural language systems, speech recognisers, and others.

1.5 MIXED INITIATIVE SYSTEMS

W e have briefly considered the need for more variation in the basic level modes of interaction between human and computer. We now consider another change, but which occurs at a higher, more conceptual level.

Fig 1.3 draws an analogy between the use of a computer and the work of a mechanic. One way of characterising the increasing sophistication of computer-based tools is to consider their status vis-a-vis their human users. The more simple systems can be regarded as very specialised tools. More complex conventional systems, perhaps employing a database, can then be seen as more powerful and general purpose tools. With the advent of knowledge-based systems, however, the system's status rises to that of partner. The important point to grasp is that whereas conventional systems can function as straightforward tools, many knowledge-based systems must assume a rather different status to be fully effective.

If one considers the interactions with the differing systems in fig 1.3, it can be seen that the systems characterised as tools will always be used in more or less the same way (depending upon their generality), and will not be expected to contribute to the consideration of alternative courses of action. Thus they may have a more or less fixed mode of interaction, which makes fixed assumptions about the user's tasks. By contrast, many knowledge-based systems require the computer and the human to work as a partnership, and this partnership will only function if both parties initiate interaction (ask questions, or set goals) and respond (answer, or carry out investigations). This two way process is known as 'mixed initiative'. Ideally, the dialogue should be as free-form as possible.

There are three pre-requisites for mixed initiative systems to function effectively. The first is that the basic mode of interaction allows it. The use of natural language is often

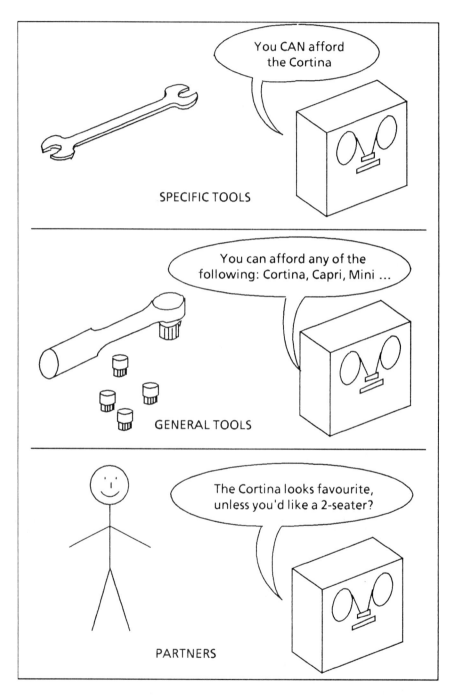

Fig 1.3   Computer systems as tools

cited as an ideal, but much can be achieved by making a wide range of options available to the user.

The second is the use of some form of user modelling by the system. The prime difficulty with programming a system to undertake mixed initiative dialogue is that the user's possible courses of action are more numerous at each point in the dialogue. Interpreting what are therefore unexpected requests is not easy without a model of the requester. To illustrate this, think back to the last time that someone you were engaged in conversation with suddenly interrupted the path of the discussion with a surprise remark. Depending upon your model of that person, you might have interpreted the remark in a number of ways, each leading to a different action:

Interpretation	Action
non sequitur	acknowledge and carry on conversation on same path
a demonstration of a lack of understanding	return to an earlier stage in the conversation and re-explain
knowledgable and relevant criticism	move along a new path suggested by the remark

The third prerequisite is that the system have some flexible and explicit representation of the tasks that it can address, and the relationships between those tasks.

A large part of this book is dedicated to explaining how knowledge-based techniques can address all of these problems more effectively than conventional approaches. Chapters 3 and 4 are devoted to this topic, but some of the ideas recur throughout the book.

1.6 EXPERT SYSTEMS DESIGN – A USER-CENTRED APPROACH

We have stressed the need to consider human factors in knowledge-based system development. However, we should always remember that neither system nor user exists in

isolation. Carey (4) sums the importance of the holistic view
thus:

> 'the crucial role of requirements analysis in software
> engineering has become axiomatic. The same
> importance should be attached to task analysis for
> interface engineering, where the emphasis is on the
> nature of the activities that the information system will
> support, rather than on the specific processing functions
> to be developed.
> Effective design of the working interface between
> humans and computers cannot merely depend upon
> catalogues of previous 'characteristics' of each of these
> two entities, nor on optimising individual functions in
> the interactions ... the entire task, including its goals, is
> therefore the proper reference for the design.'

It is necessary to specifically address the mis-match
between the designer's model of the task and system, and the
user's models of the two, and to consider the particular user.

The models (and the resulting mis-matches) become
increasingly complex in IKBSs, where not only might the user
have a model of task and system, but the system may have a
model of the user. Furthermore, both models may change, and
not necessarily in harmony.

To resolve this mis-match the designer must understand the
user's needs, ensure that a full job description is available, and
ensure that any compromises do not impinge on the the user's
'expectation boundaries' (in other words, the minimal
acceptable system).

There are many approaches to task and requirements
analysis. Whilst we will later consider approaches to
knowledge acquisition in detail, it is worthwhile exploring
some general principles of good design. Long (5) proposes the
model of activities associated with the system development
paradigm shown in fig 1.4.

Long's approach demonstrates how different areas
contribute to the overall development of a system. Whilst the
model is incomplete, it shows clearly the value of a multi-
layered model of the development process, with each layer
being in some way essential to the development. It also
illustrates the different views and perspectives which can be

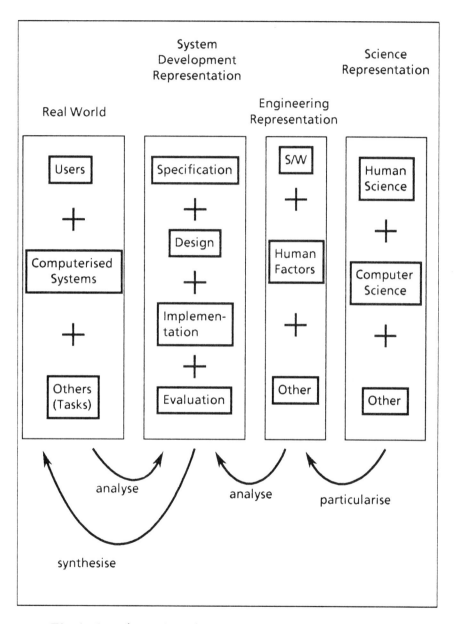

Fig 4   Long's model of system development activities

put upon the same problem and the need for multi-roles in the design process.

The most important feature of Long's model is that it allows a number of different roles and approaches to contribute to the development of a system.

1.7 CONCLUSIONS

We will explore many strands of Ergonomics, IKBSs and system design. However, the underlying theme of this book is the inter-relationships between these areas. The need to consider the user at all stages and the large number of factors which contribute to the eventual success of the system will also be highlighted. This book is of use for those involved in human factors, AI and related subjects; those who manage the new technologies; and those who simply want to know more about the field. It is essentially a practical book, drawing heavily on existing systems and practice. It documents both successes and failures of the new technology and builds a framework for working with IKBSs.

1.8 REFERENCES

1. Weizenbaum J, (1976), 'Computer Power and Human Reason,' San Francisco, W. H. Freeman

2. Frudes N, (1983), 'The intimate machine,' Century

3. For further details about the VODIS project, contact the Alvey Directorate, Kingsgate House, 66-74 Victoria St, London, SW1E 6SW

4. Carey T, 'Dialogue handling with user workstations,' Proc. Interact '84, Elsevier Science

5. Long, 'People and Computers: designing for usability', Proc. of 'People and computers: designing for usability', HCI '86, York, ed. Harrison and Mish

2

Input and interaction

2.1 INTRODUCTION

This chapter examines the developments in methods of input, assessing both their continuing influence on the development of computer systems and the consequences new methods of input may have for recently developed IKBS techniques.

To understand the influence of input mechanisms it is important to be aware of how they have already played a key role in the development of past and current systems. We should also realise that the developing user awareness of the consequences of using input methods will lead to fundamental changes in design.

Until recently the only way to communicate with a computer has been via a keyboard. Different types of keyboard and intermediaries - ranging from punched card to paper tape - have been used. Nevertheless, input has always involved somebody sitting down and typing at some stage.

This picture has been changing. Developments in touch and pointing devices, the application of AI techniques to voice and handwriting recognition, are all affecting the way in which we communicate with the computer. Each method has its pros and cons and no one method can be considered universal. Indeed, it seems unlikely that we will ever develop a truly universal input method. However, as the input devices become more varied so have the applications, often shaped by the devices until the two become impossible to divorce. Debates about which device is best have produced experiments, elegantly designed to conclusively prove the superiority of one device over others, but merely showing the dependence of one device upon the application it has been used for.

The aim of this chapter is to outline the problems of each device and the areas where it will be or has been of most use. Finally, it will summarise how, by integrating the devices, systems can be produced which will be significantly better than those which have gone before.

The human-computer interface is generally the key to the success or failure of a system. How well the computer communicates with the user and vice-versa is the limiting factor on the effectiveness of the system. Both computers and users have a limited range of ways in which they can communicate. Humans are further limited by the number of channels of information they are able to deal with in real time. A good description of the human as a system component and the physiological and psychological capabilities of the human as an information processor can be found in (5). This includes a summary of vision, taste, audition, vibration and electrical shock as methods of stimulus plus examination of man as a single or multi-channel operator. Whilst it is not the purpose of this book to explore these issues, it is important to note that the choice of input or output mechanisms has very specific consequences for the user's performance. For example, the choice of auditor output will provide immediate attention getting information which, however, is unlikely to be retained.

2.2 THE KEYBOARD

The most frequently used keyboard was developed by Shoales in the nineteenth century. It is commonly called the QWERTY keyboard. The design was such that key clashes (which resulted in jammed keyboards) were minimised. To achieve this, so it is claimed, the keyboard was designed to slow the user down and to ensure that keys which should be pressed virtually together, were not. Another feature of the design is the uneven emphasis it places on each hand (and on each finger). A debate has been raging since as to how best to design keyboards. Advocates have variously supported Dvorak's design, the simplified keyboard and the chord keyboard. Whole professions have been established around the keyboard - typists, audio-typists and data entry clerks. The only point that all observers have agreed on is that typing is a highy skilled task. It is not natural for most of us and to become a good typist it is necessary to learn a new skill. A summary of the major issues in the design of keyboards can be found in a PhD carried out at the Human Sciences and Advanced Technology (HUSAT) reasearch centre by J. Martin (1).

The computer, and more specifically the micro-computer, has produced a new breed of typists - the 'hunt and peck' user. These are individuals who have never learned how to type with more than a couple of fingers, who must search out each key by sight and who rarely achieve typing speeds of more than 15 words per minute. It is significant that even very experienced computer users are mostly 'hunt and peck' typists.

A computer system is generally very dependent on information being input. Since programmers are highly skilled in their own field but not in typing, two trends have emerged. As programmers are driven by the need for minimum key-strokes (and remembering that programmers take no longer to find and press unusual or obscure keys than normal keys), it becomes easy to invent conventions which would be hard for a normal typist to input at speed, but which cost the programmer no additional time and save on keystrokes. Also, abbreviations become rampant e.g. a much misunderstood UNIX abbreviation 'cat', used to output a file, is actually an abbreviation for the much longer word, concatenate. Almost all operating systems contain a host of obscure abbreviations which serve to baffle the naive user and confuse users experienced in different systems.

Another key issue in the use of keyboards is starting to emerge in Australia. There is a tendency for heavy users of keyboards to appear to develop Repetitive Strain Injury (RSI). This disease is not confined to keyboard users nor to the arms and hands, but is a feature of any task which over emphasises the use of one particular limb or muscle. However, the RSI scare has become linked with the keyboard and with high pressure, high speed data input and it might have a significant effect on the introduction of new, keyboard oriented technology. This is in spite of the fact that it seems that RSI is not directly attributable to the keyboard (in a recent court action, an Australian court decided that there was not a case to answer). Nevertheless, RSI continues to be a controversial issue in Australia, and this creates the possibility that it will emerge elsewhere in the next few years. It is not clear why it is so prevalent in just one country, and there is as yet no theory to explain the prevalence of RSI.

It is soon apparent that developments over the last 20 years have been significantly influenced, and to some extent hampered, by developments which had occurred during the previous century. It is not surprising that there has been a move (largely manufacturer driven) away from the keyboard as the sole means of input to, and interaction with, the computer. This movement has coincided with the development of more sophisticated systems. The coining of phrases such as 'user friendly' and 'natural interaction' is synonomous with these changes.

Undoubtably keyboards have had, and will continue to have, a significant impact on system design. Whether this will lead to the development of better systems, or systems which are genuinely easy to use for naive and inexperienced users, is not yet clear.

2.3 POINTING DEVICES

First attempts to solve some of the problems attributed to keyboards probably started with the introduction of light pens and touch sensistive screens. Users were able to escape the limitations of the keyboard through employing either pointing devices or through using their fingers. Although a variety of novel input devices were available, pointing was the first to see widespread use.

2.3.1 Touch

Touch sensitive screen rely on the user interacting with the system by pointing at objects on the screen. One of the most obvious disadvantages of touch sensitive screens which rely on the user touching the screen with a finger is that fingers are not very good pointing devices. They are stubby and grubby. Users often lack co-ordination, especially if they are required to point many times. The accumulated grim and grease has a tendency to move from the finger onto the screen and the screen becomes more difficult to read. Similarly, there are problems with parallax and the user's inability to point at the right area.

There have been attempts to solve the problem, such as developments in non-contact touch screens, where the user's finger breaks an infra-red beam located above the plane of the screen. Unfortunately such devices tend to exaggerate the problems of parallax and users may not always get what they think they are touching on the screen.

The touch sensitive screen provides a good example of how the input device determines the characteristic of the interaction. Such devices work best on menus - it is simpler for inexperienced users to point to what they want rather than to type it (even if only one letter is required). Thus, if studies are done comparing the efficacy of touch-screens, it is found that they triumph in systems which are primarily menu driven. This result may be confusing. Whilst the system might be better driven by touch, the underlying design might not be ideal i.e. if the system could be better designed, menus might not be the appropriate form of interaction. Hence, instead of separating the overall design process into two stages (underlying design and mode of interaction), it may be necessary to compare different designs in conjunction with their most suitable mode of interaction.

A very practical example of this occurs in the Prestel system. Users perform better (ie faster and with fewer errors) if they use touch. Unfortunately this does not mean that the system only needs a touch sensitive screen to make it easy to use. The underlying design has many faults (eg it is too heavily dependent upon hierarchical menus) and these underlying faults must be addressed first, with the result that in a new system touch might not be the most appropriate form of user interaction.

The significance of this is that if we are designing the interface to advanced systems, we should be careful not to let the method of input dominate the design of the system. In general touch can be used where the system is menu based and the user will not have to point to the screen many times (thus reducing issues such as fatigue). Touch is a method of interacting with a computer which requires little in the way of special skills, and as such is ideal for naive users. It will not be as good for experienced users, who might not want to have to take their hands off the keyboard. Also, the designer should not overlook the problems which result from dirty screens, parallax and the tendency of users to drop their fingers (ie to point to just under the area they intend to point to).

It is hard to determine which is the best way of designing a touch screen. Infra-red systems have advantages for experienced users (who will not touch the screen as often or as hard) whilst touch sensitive grids allow more areas to be defined and greater accuracy (providing the user's fingers are not too stubby!).

In general, the areas which the system is monitoring for specific cues should be large enough and separate enough to ensure that incorrect signals are minimised.

2.3.2 Light pens

Many of the points made for touch senstive screens are applicable to light pens (though they should not make the screen as dirty). Users are likely to be less adept at pointing with a light-pen than with a finger but are likely to be able to perform more sensitive operations, especially if used in conjunciton with a tablet. This facility can be used to great advantage in some systems. For example, the Applicon workstation is frequently used in the design of VLSI chips. There is simply no way a keyboard can be as efficiently used as a light pen and tablet to perform some drawing motions.

The Applicon system also has one other feature - the user is able to define strings of functions as single pen movements. This allows frequently used complex commands to become single figures drawn with the light pen. This feature is the equivalent to writing macros in some computer systems but has an elegance and aesthetic quality which far surpasses multi-key or multi-shift presses.

This system highlights a developing trend in systems which is an important consideration in all IKBS systems. If a system is intelligent enough, the user will wish to use more simple commands in a more 'natural' way to perform complex tasks.

For example, if a user wishes to draw a rectangle, then inputing four co-ordinate pairs via the keyboard is probably acceptable. Conversely, if drawing a house, then some other form of input (such as a graphics tablet) becomes a necessity.

There are obvious problems with this approach – eg how does the user remember what figure is equivalent to which command string – but the facility seems to far outweigh the problems which it causes.

2.3.3 Mice and tracker ball systems

Light pens and touch screens represent fairly conventional methods of interaction, translated into computer terms. A light pen is an extention of a normal pen – whether it is used to write or to point – and pointing with fingers is a well rehearsed skill.

It was only in the last decade that a number of new input technologies have been widely used which were not directly analogous to common methods of communication.

The first of these novel devices is the mouse. Despite being first developed by the Stanford Research Institute in the 1960s, the idea was not commercially exploited for almost a decade. It required a number of hardware and software developments before the mouse reached pre-eminence in the late 1970s and early 1980s. The majority of systems utilising mice also incorporate other elements in a full WIMP (Windows, Icons, Mice and Pointing) system – see later.

The mouse evolved from the tracker-ball. This was a device which had found a military use for several years but was not common in commercial systems. The tracker-ball allowed the user to move around the screen far more easily and freely than could be obtained using cursor keys. It also appeared to be a more natural form of interaction. Users apparently have little or no trouble in moving from one part of the screen to another using the tracker-ball (though they may overshoot or undershoot and need to corrct). A tracker-ball allowed the user to move to a spot far more quickly than through the use of keys and users had little problem with the device. Unfortunately, tracker-balls result in large keyboards. They have to be large devices to allow users to accurately move and position the cursor. Hence, they have a tendency to be rather cumbersome, and not everybody likes them.

One attempt to solve some of the problems with the tracker-ball was the touch-sensitive pad. This was a pad located to the side of the keyboard which the user pressed to move the cursor around. These pads were touch and pressure sensitive. The harder the user pressed, the faster the cursor moved in the selected direction. This system too had many problems. The users were often required to be too discriminating in how hard they had to press the pad and in which location. This lead to errors of undershoot/overshoot and the subsequent problems in getting the cursor lined up.

One of the first systems to get away from this approach, though still using a tracker ball, was the Xerox Star. However, the Star not only used the tracker ball, but designed the system around it, thus becoming the first of the new generation of systems whose design has been determined by the means of interaction.

Xerox exploited a pointing device called a mouse. This was simply an inverted tracker ball, the ball being a ball-bearing, located on the underside of a large plastic shell. The user moved the shell and the cursor followed. In some systems the mouse is controlled by its own processor, to ensure that it moves at the same speed as the user, providing immediate feedback. In others, the user must move the mouse then wait for the system to respond.

The mouse was seen as a remote pointing device, rather like a light pen on a tablet, where the user moves the pen and something happens on the screen. As the mouse is a fairly bulky device it was difficult to accomplish complex movements (eg writing is an extremely difficult business, as recent studies at the National Physical Laboratories have highlighted). Thus the device was seen as a method of moving a cursor about and pointing to an area. The mouse also has a variable number of buttons (usually from one to four) which allow the user to perform a range of manoeuvres without use of the keyboard.

Alone this feature is not very useful. However, when combined with the right system, a mouse driven cursor can produce results to beat any other input mechanism (2). The right interface appears to be the use of the WIMP-style interface described earlier, along with, in many cases, pop-up or pull-down menus.

A window is an area of a display which is discrete from all other areas (see fig 2.1). A mouse can generally be used to open it, close it, move it, change its size or its function simply by moving a cursor and clicking a button or buttons located on top of the mouse (fig 2.1).

The WIMP interface also requires a screen with graphics capability. This will preferably be high resolution (at least 70 pixels per inch) though often cost dictates lower quality (for example, most PCs). Items of interest within the system are represented as pictures, known as 'icons'. These icons represent a range of system functions, from shrunken menus to waste-paper baskets. Icons are selected by pointing with the mouse, can be rearranged by selecting and dragging with the mouse, or disposed of into a waste paper basket. It is interesting to note the extent to which icons have taken over the displays of all kinds of system. There appears to be a prevailing belief amongst system designers that icons are *de facto* a good idea and always represent a more usable system. Often the icons are far from the best representation for the item they represent. Work by Browne and Stammers (3) has illustrated that simple redesign can produce better results. This is because icons are often intuitively designed by only one person whose terms of reference may be very different from those of the user (in expert systems terms, consider the gulf between expert consultant and client).

Much of the debate related to mouse driven systems has been around one, two, three, etc button mice, whether windows should be allowed to overlap, and which icons are equivalent to which functions. There has been litte consideration as to whether such systems are fundamentally a good idea. The most likely reason for this is that such systems are so much better than anything previously available that it is difficult to critically assess the fundamental design principles underlying them. So, the debate rages as to whether users should be allowed to create an electronically untidy desk, but not as to whether window/icon/mice systems are a good idea - as far as system builders are concerned, they obviously are. Studies comparing mice with touch panels and keyboards tend to study a small part of the overall problem. For example, Karat et al (4) looked at target selection and produced significant advantages for touch and keyboard input, whilst

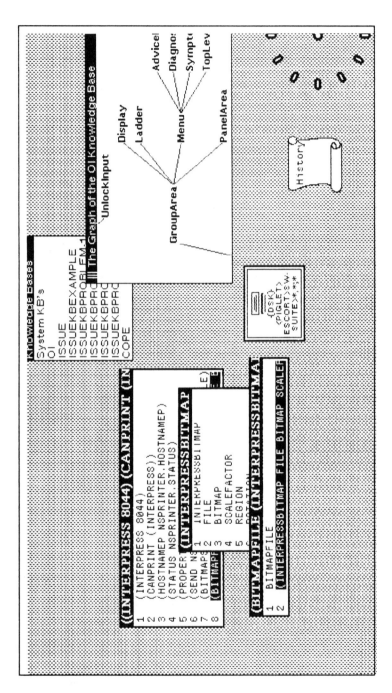

Figure 2.1   Example window display

Card et al (2) found that for their task (text selection) mice represented the best method of input. It appears that the results of the experiment are determined by how you design your task or which application you are studying. Once again, the practice of comparing modes of interaction in isolation is seen to be inadequate.

This should not disguise the fundamental advantage that WIMP systems often possess. They generally are used with software designed to benefit from such an approach. These systems will produce better results overall, in terms of ease of use, frequency of errors, etc. than systems which have been constructed in a more haphazard way. However, it is the integration, rather than the input device which produces the success. In many cases, other approaches, using other input technology will produce acceptable results, provided that the device has affected the system design.

2.4 SPEECH INPUT

Speech input has been one of the technologies to benefit most from developments in AI. Speech recognisers have been developed in isolation at the same time as touch systems. However, such devices were often crude, performing simple pattern matching, hamstrung by fundamental problems with the algorithms, the hardware and the software. As such, they have not found widespread acceptance and speech recognisers have generally only been used in limited application areas, such as `hands busy' situations (eg inside the cockpit of an aircraft).

The issues associated with speech recognisers are more complex than those associated with other input devices. As with other devices, ease of use, accuracy and training times are just as important as ensuring that the technology is appropriate and affordable. However, the assessment of speech recognisers is a serious problem, as is the likely effect the technology will have when introduced on a large scale. This section will consider some of the issues peculiar to speech recognition which are fundamental to its success.

The options available to system designers are many and complex. Should a system operate with discrete or continuous speech ? How much time does the user have to spend inputting the basic vocabulary and training the system (both of which can represent significant overheads) ?   The designer must consider the problem of cognitive dissonance (a theme which is expanded on in Chapter 5). It is likely to be a major source of difficulty if the user's model of the system does not match the system's model of the user, especially if the user believes that the system is understanding rather than recognising speech.

The problem of speaker dependence or independence will influence the applications the device will be suitable for, especially if it is to be used in a non-specialised environment. Finally, the applications and future developments of the system must be considered.

2.4.1 Discrete versus continuous recognition

One of the fundamental questions applied to speech recognition systems is whether the system should be capable of recognising discrete or continuous speech. In other words, should the system require the user to pause (even if only for a fraction of a second) between words or phrases or should the system be capable of recognising natural speech. Natural speech contains many inconsistences, co-articulations and rhythms, making the recognition task extremely complex. Fig 2.2 illustrates some of the problems. Most workers would generally agree that the ultimate goal is continuous recognition. Users should be capable of communicating naturally with the system, with minimum modification to their speech (and hopefully their behaviour). There seems to be an underlying belief that continuous recognition is a significant step towards speech understanding.

2.4.2 Training

The early speech recognition systems required full training. The user had to provide one, or, more often, several examples of how a particular word or phrase was spoken. This allowed the system to store several examples or construct composite patterns describing each word.

The applications for this technology were limited. For example, one Government application - digitising maps using a speech recogniser to input the digits - required the user to retrain the whole system frequently (several times a day) if performance was to be maintained. This is acceptable if the

1. Inconsistent pronunciation

> eg moving from north to south in Britain, one might hear 'Bath' pronounced firstly 'Barth' and secondly'Bahth'

2. Co-articulation

> eg the running together of sounds: '2, 8, 10' is likely to be spoken as 'two eigh ten'

3. Rhythms

> eg a voice tends to trail off at the end of a sentence

Fig 2.2 Some of the problems with recognition of continuous speech

user is prepared to do it and the vocabulary is small. If the vocabulary is not 10-20 words but 10-20 thousand words it becomes less practical. Talkwriters - voice driven word processors - will have vocabularies this large. If a user's voice alters and the system performance falls there might be a requirement to input some 60,000 words. Even if performance can be maintained once the initial patterns are input this may still be an unexceptably high overhead. Systems with medium size vocabularies (1,000 words) have run into problems. In one case a user attempted to input some 600 words in one session. By the end of the session he had provided nearly 2000 examples of the words. His voice had so changed during the course of the training that later attempts to use the system were very error prone. Not only had the initial training session been inconvenient and time consuming; it was also largely a waste of time as many of the words needed retraining in a more 'normal' voice. It is for this reason that performance of recognition systems has often been poor when the systems have moved from the lab into the office. Similarly, if a system has been trained by a user in an unstressed environment, performance is likely to deteriorate when the user provides a demonstration to a large audience.

The solution to these 'tough trained' systems is to devise a method which requires the user to provide only a small sample of the stored words. The system is then able to construct a model of how other words will be pronounced based on this sample – 'the easy trained' approach. The first systems capable of easy training have been developed by IBM and SSI.

An easy trained system does not rely on pattern patching on the word level, but operates on the phoneme or equivalent level. Ideally between 50 and 500 sounds are used to build the words. A user must provide a sample of each sound and is generally required to provide the system with about 300 words (sometimes slightly more, if the system is a continuous recogniser).

A further problem is that which occurs when different words have the same pronunciation (see fig 2.3). In such situations, the only solution is the use of AI techniques borrowed from natural language processing research (see Chapter 4). This means, however, that the training of the system now requires some input of grammar rules, rather akin to programming the system.

2.4.3 Speaker Indepence versus Speaker Dependence

Some systems will be required to deal with more than one speaker. The simplest way to do this is to require samples of each individual's speech and to pattern match. However some systems (for example, the Verbex system) are able to recognise speech without the requirement of a previous sample. For example one recognition system might be able to recognise digits over a telephone when spoken discretely, with high accuracy. However, the system's ability will be based on a large collection of samples of different people saying the digits used to produce several composite patterns. The degree of variation that the system will deal with will depend ultimately on the range of the samples on which it is based.

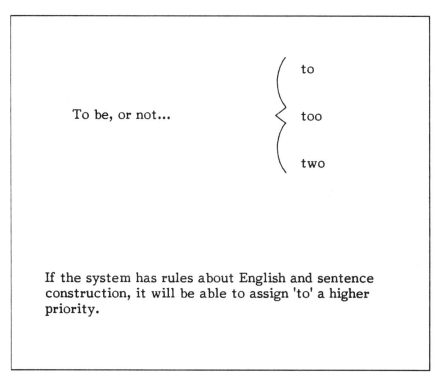

To be, or not...

    to

    too

    two

If the system has rules about English and sentence construction, it will be able to assign 'to' a higher priority.

Fig 2.3   Which word to choose ?

2.4.4 Future Developments

Many techniques have been employed in developing speech recognition systems.   Some are simple pattern matching , others rely on vast databases of words and probabilities of word strings occuring together (eg the IBM system), whilst knowledge about semantics, parsers and other speech rules have all been used to improve recognition performance. Incorporating the most sophisticated recognition techniques with developments in Natural Language understanding (see Chapter 4) will move speech recognisers from simple recognition towards speech understanding.

1987/88 should see the introduction of large vocabulary (>10,000 words), easy trained (<500 words), cheap (<$2,000) systems.   Hopefully some of the issues raised in this section will have been addressed.   Even so, it is likely that most systems will have been produced largely in-vacuo.   The technology will be in search of an application with mass market appeal. A few systems will provide exceptions, being developed for a particular application eg VODIS, but the majority will be aimed at general solutions to specific problems, especially if speech is to be introduced into the office.

Already people have problems using Dictaphones, and with free-flow composition. Human secretaries have the intelligence to deal with hesitations, pauses and repetitions, but it may be some while before talkwriters do. Similarly, error correction will be a severe problem even though non-recognition systems, such as the Palantype (see Newell (6)), have shown how intelligent editors can be developed. These editors (aimed at solving the propagation problems with continuous recognisers) are able to use knowledge about an error in the past to correct errors in the future which have propagated from that point.

2.5 HANDWRITING RECOGNITION

This method of input is in many ways analogous to speech recognition. The underlying statistical methods (eg Hidden Markov Modelling) apply equally to speech and to writing recognition. The same problems occur - writer dependency, the need for training, error rates, etc.

However, this particular input method shows very clearly the inter-dependence of technologies. Almost all handwriting recognition systems will be based on something which will be equivalent to paper ie it will rest on the desk, should be portable, convenient to use, etc.

It is hard to conceive of a system which requires the user to input data in anything other than a natural, handwriting form ie writing with the pen in the vertical position. This would imply that ideally the system should employ something like a flat screen.

Again, the system will utilise AI techniques to improve performance and should prove the ideal front-end to many AI systems, where complex graphic and text input is required. As with the light-pen, already used on some advanced workstations, the system will offer substantial advantages as an input method.

The technical problems which occur with handwriting recognition are similar to those with speech.   Whilst co-articulation is not a problem, it will be hard to build a system which will be writer independent or even capable of dealing with all the variations in individuals' handwriting (consider the chemist and the doctor's prescription - it will be difficult to construct a system which will perform as well as a human, at least in the short term).   There will probably be less market reluctance to purchase handwriting recognisers, as opposed to speech recognisers.   This is because handwriting recognisers can be directly substituted into the office, replacing current writing or drawing tasks.   Also, the problem which speech will create in the socio-technical organisation of the office will be less pronounced for handwriting.

Handwriting recognition systems are currently under development.   They need to be designed as part of a more complex system but offer substantial advantages as an input method.

2.6 AS AI COMES OF AGE - THE NEED FOR MULTI-MODALITY

Having reviewed the major forms of input, including some which are still not widespread, it is important to consider the general implications of the devices, and to see how they relate to developments of other systems.

Newer developments in input devices have far-reaching implications.   Voice input and handwriting input will impact the office, perhaps modifying or even eliminating some jobs.

The type of input device used affects the look of the system, altering designs and influencing use.   As these input devices are generally built before the application, then often the application serves to optimise the device, rather than the device optimising the application.

Developments in AI are having two main effects:

• They are enabling more sophisticated devices to be developed.

• They are allowing the development of more flexible and complex applications.

The real influence of the various input devices will occur when they are used in conjunction with well designed systems that they match well. AI techniques will help enable this, for example when used in intelligent front-ends combined with voice. A system should not be dependent upon one particular method of input nor should an application. Rather, the input method should be user definable, flexible and well matched to the application.

It will be of little use to offer an intelligent front-end, accessible through a keyboard only to find that the user cannot type. Similarly, to consider one particular input method as better than all others and usable in all circumstances is naive and dangerous. If the main aim of system designers is usability (and it ought to be), then they must ensure that the method or better still the range of methods for communication with the system matches the applications.

2.7 CHOOSING INPUT DEVICES FOR EXPERT SYSTEMS

This section will attempt to address the question of whether expert systems favour any particular device to a greater extent than most conventional systems. To answer this, one should start by making some generalisations about expert systems.

Firstly, interaction with an expert system is much more two-way than with a conventional system. Indeed, with more advanced consultation systems, the flow of information is of equal size in both directions. This contrasts sharply with the situation in most conventional systems. Secondly, because the expert system deals in more vague terms than the average system, there will be a definite need for the user to be able to express quite complex ideas.

This need is reflected in systems which attempt to deal with uncertainty. Here the user must express the idea of how certain or uncertain a fact is. The system makes demands on the user which necessitate the user interacting with the system in a different way from the normal, prescriptive way. There may be no right or wrong answers, but instead just answers which will convey degrees of information.

A major part of the human-computer interaction is the ability to ask for and receive explanations of an expert system's reasoning. This involves presenting parts of the system's knowledge base to the user, and the internal representation and structure of that knowledge should be reflected.

Thirdly, there is a greater need to protect against cognitive dissonance. A user is much more likely to form an inaccurate model of how an expert system works for two reasons: firstly, it is often very complex, and secondly, it performs tasks normally associated with humans. Because of this, the user is much more likely to be misled by preconceptions about 'the obvious way to do this'.

Considering these points as a whole, two ideas emerge. Firstly, a user entering large quantities of data, often judgemental (and thus expressed linguistically) is unlikely to be happy with typing. The ideal is likely to be speech: failing this, the system builder should design a system to allow the user to construct large structures from smaller parts using a minimum of keystrokes, and graphical representations are likely to be particularly effective in this endeavour.

The second idea springs from the need for the system to 'explain itelf'. To do this, it needs a powerful output mechanism. Once again graphics may be useful, particularly for describing information or knowledge about material items. The output should ideally be similar to the input devices.

The role that input devices have played in defining the system must be decreased in favour of systems which are defined by the user's needs and the problems which the user-system team is attempting to solve. The idea of making the input device fit the user's needs is a theme reflected throughout the book. It is now becoming possible to view the user and the computer as more than just black boxes. Complex theories of human-computer interaction can explore the possibilities and problems associated with the range of input devices which are becoming available.

The right choice of input method enables the user to interpret information more easily. For example, graphical information can convey more easily certain information to both the user and the computer.

The choice of input device has been influenced in the past by the design of the whole system. The keyboard has dictated that information be entered at a maximum rate (determined by the physiological capabilities, training, skill, etc. of the operator), whilst the limiting factor on WIMP interfaces is the adequacy of their representations to facilitate the interaction. Similarly, the newer technologies impact the form of the system, and even the surrounding environment – for example, speech recognition may not be able to cope with the noisy office, which may affect both office design and working practices.

2.8 CONCLUSIONS

This chapter has specifically concentrated on input. We have not discussed output methods other than windowing systems, as they have had less impact on the design of systems. We have illustrated that performance is not dependent upon a device but rather on how the whole system has been designed. IKBSs can benefit in particular ways from the use of new input devices but the introduction of these devices will not, per se, produce better systems.

2.9 REFERENCES

1. Martin J M, (1978) 'A literature review of knowledge based research', HUSAT Memo 164

2. Card S K, English W K and Burr B J, (1978) 'Evaluation of mouse, rate-controlled isometric joystick, step keys, and text keys for text selection on a CRT,' Ergonomics, 21, 601-613

3. Browne R M and Stammers R B, (1987), 'The evaluation and generation of icons for a computer drawing package,' Proc. Ergonomics Annual Conference, Taylor and Francis

4. Karat J et al, (1984), 'A comparison of selection techniques: touch panel, mouse and keyboard,' Proc Interact '84, Elsevier Science

5. Van Cott H P and Kinkade R G, (1972), 'Human Engineering Guide to Equipment Design,' McGraw-Hill

6. Newell A F, (1984), 'Speech – the natural modality for man-machine interaction ?,' Proc. Interact '84, Elsevier Science

3

Modes of interaction and dialogue design

3.1 INTRODUCTION

The previous chapter has concentrated on the design of hardware, the range of input devices which are available and how those devices have influenced the design of systems. However, the hardware is only one aspect of the interaction between the human, the interface and the machine.

In this chapter we move some way towards resolving the problems which occur at the interface by trying to understand the user and the machine, rather than by considering the hardware tools in use.

Firstly, we examine the characteristics of Human-Computer Interaction in most modern computer systems. We consider how these conflict with the way in which most people think and operate, and how poor design, per se, will lead to errors and disaffection. Alternative forms of interaction are considered which address this problem to a greater or lesser extent. The various solutions are evaluated against three criteria:

- the benefits they present to the user

- the problems which they attempt to solve

- the problems they cause.

Methods of achieving these new forms of interaction are described and a number of issues involved in the various forms of 'user modelling' are discussed.

Apart from considering the system's model of the user, we also consider the user's model of the system. We outline why it is important and how different user models affect system use. A number of theoretical models are presented which attempt to explain the different types of models which users construct.

This chapter also examines the problems and benefits of adaptiveness - from both a system and a user perspective. The need for mixed-initative dialogue is illustrated, by consideration of systems which are computer driven or user driven. Lastly, the roles which such systems can play in the design of IKBSs are considered.

The chapter will take as an example the presentation of computer programs to the system. Ths will serve to illustrate the problems associated with the presentation of data in general. A program is highly representative of structured, specific information designed to fulfill a certain task in a specific way (hopefully defined by the user).

Before we consider the problem in detail it is important to consider exactly what certain terms mean, and what are the perspectives they provide on certain problems.

The major divisions are between user and computer. The term user model is used specifically to describe the model of the user which resides inside the computer system. All computer systems have such a model; it may only reside implicitly within the program code, and be completely un-modifiable, but it nvertheless is there.

In addition, the user will have a model of the system. This is the model that the user empioys to structure his/her interaction with the system. This will be affected by the designer's model of the system, and how the designer intended the user to perceive the system.

Finally there is an idealised model of the overall system, which assumes that both computer and user have perfect knowledge and interact co-operatively.

The relationships between the differing models are summarised in fig 3.1.

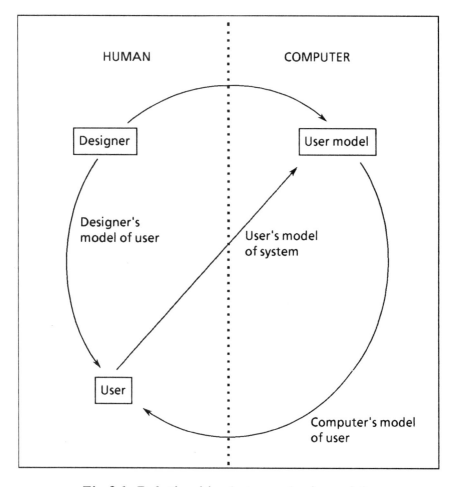

Fig 3.1 Relationships between basic models

3.2 INTERACTION - THE DOMINANT ROLE OF THE MACHINE

In the past, interaction across the interface has been dominated by the machine. In the previous chapters we described how users have been forced to foreshorten the wide range of communication mechanisms available to them when they use machines. It is only rarely that users have been able to employ the full range of possibilities - speech, touch, movement, etc. - to communicate with the computer. This is only one of two problems. The other is the level at which the communication occurs. Not only has the communication been restricted but the user has been forced to communicate with the machine at a very low level. The interaction demanded by the computer has been highly structured and restrictive. The system has been intolerant of errors and ignorance; the user has been required to formulate obscure commands in an unusual language which might be nothing more than a collection of letters and numbers.

The artificial nature of this interaction has caused the user problems. In describing the level of abstraction at which the interaction takes place it becomes possible to describe the computer system. Indeed, from the user's viewpoint the level of interaction with the user and its abstraction from detail might be the dominant feature of how useable the system is. Thus, at the lowest level the user is forced to communicate in the only terms the computer will understand - a collection of 1's and 0's. Advancing from this, assemblers offer more consideration for the user, though great skill is still required. Commands can be employed to run assembler routines and might even offer the user a chance of employing a meaningful word. This schema can be extended to the point where the user requires a complex solution to a complex problem and simply instructs the computer about the problem, in the terms which the user finds easiest and most natural.

From a human factors standpoint, the progress from machine code, to assemblers, through third generation and then fourth generation computer languages reflects an underlying trend in the design of systems. The move is away from detailed level procedural instructions towards goal-directed, high-level behaviour. Seen thus, the fifth generation of systems should exhibit a greater understanding of the user and operate in a goal-directed manner. It is no longer sufficient to consider the interaction in terms of small, specific sub-problems which the users are required to define and take account of. Systems need to operate by defining larger problems, sometimes taking a backseat in defining the route to a solution. The computer should neither be allowed nor required to drive the interaction except where genuinely appropriate. The user should be allowed an input. One of the most exciting prospects of expert systems and the development of IKBSs is that they have the potential to allow the nature of the interface to change in this way. The user can be better understood and catered for, and the computer can be allowed to form only one part of the human-computer interface.

In summary, there have been two major recurrent problems in the high level design of human-computer interfaces. The first major problem is that the vast majority of interaction has been dominated by the system. This is true even of command language systems, where the user's domination is only superficial.

The second major problem is that computers have required the user to specify the problem in too much detail. System functions, and thus user commands, have been at too low level in terms of the overall problem domain. The user has been forced to string many complex and meaningless commands together to perform even simple tasks. This is especially a problem when the user cannot see that the task requires sub-dividing. If the issue appears simple, then the solution also should be and, most importantly, the method of arriving at that solution should be. A user does not expect to have to write an assembler routine to multiply two numbers together. Similarly, a user should not be required to perform half a dozen keystrokes to delete one letter from a document which is being word processed.

These problems are significant for a number of reasons. Firstly, the more operations required to complete a task, the more opportunities the user has to make errors. A common characteristic of all human-computer interaction is that it is rarely error free. Both programmers and users are fond of telling people that nothing ever works first time - be it a single program or a system. This is an alarming comment, especially when applied to multi-million dollar systems. A good example is the US's Strategic Defence Initiative. This problem is going to become more acute as systems get larger and the problems they are addressing become more complex.

Apart from the difficulties users face in operating complex systems properly, a further problem is the difficulty of ensuring that the systems themselves function correctly. Indeed, Parnas of Victoria University, uses the argument that the correct operation of all systems is impossible to verify to justify his belief that the US's Strategic Defence Initiative will not work. (1) documents a number of examples to highlight his argument that no complex system which relies on programmers and systems will ever work first time. As the SDI system will only be used once, it cannot be tested, therefore it is useless. Whether or not you agree with the argument, it highlights an area of great concern and is a problem which needs to be adressed in any large or complex system - how to get the system to work. The problem of getting a system working reliably is just as important for small systems and the arguments are equally valid whether they relate to systems or trivial tasks within a system.

A third problem is caused by the requirement of most systems to be spoon-fed problems in small chunks. Users are required to divide problems into components which often bear little resemblance to the users' understanding of the underlying task. The need to do this imposes a mechanistic way of thought on the user which is a poor match with the way that users actually tackle problems. Even providing aids to achieve this, such as flow diagrams and structured programming, does not solve the problem. The computer requires information to be represented in a specific form, otherwise it cannot be 'understood' by the computer. This form bears little relationship to the user's view of the problem; the user is forced to make all the movement required for a 'meeting of minds'.

Humans tend to exhibit goal directed behaviour. They formulate a goal and then produce a plan to achieve that goal. If the goal is too large or too long term, they split the goal into a number of sub-goals. Each sub-goal has associated plans and when the sub-goals are completed, so is the goal. Complex goals are difficult to work towards and require much planning. However, individuals have no clear ideas as to what constitutes a complex goal - different people have different perceptions about any given problem. To illustrate this consider how an experienced programmer might write a routine to find the mean of a string of numbers. It would be a trivial task requiring simple addition of inputted numbers, division and outputting the result. This same problem is often given to undergraduate psychology students and represents a week's work!

The computer mimics humans to some extent in requiring complex goals to be broken down into more understandable chunks. Unfortunately, the system's 'perception' of what constitutes a simple task is a much smaller and more tightly defined bundle of work than a human's. The problem is exacerbated by the system's inability to split the task up for itself. Thus, as has been seen earlier, a system will require a user to describe the overall goal in terms of a number of small goals which are so far removed from the original problem as to be meaningless in terms of it. In calculating the mean it might be obvious to both the psychology student and the expert programmer that the only information required is the numbers input. However, how this information is collected, used and the results output, whilst trivial to the expert, poses a considerable problem to the naive student.

In a similar way, it might be obvious to the expert user that a particular command executed in one part of a system performs one operation and that same command, if used elsewhere, will cause something different to happen. Most users will be baffled. They do not understand the underlying system structure, and it is this information which is required if the system's operation is to be understood. It requires a conceptual leap for the naive or unfamiliar computer user to see how to operate the system. Indeed, it is questionable whether they should be required to do so. Systems need not be designed for use by experts only.

3.3 INTERACTION – THE MOVE AWAY FROM THE COMPUTER

We have seen that an important characteristic of a computer system is the level of the system's goals. The way in which the user communicates with the system is determined by the level the system occupies in the user's goal tree. Imagining the user's goal described in terms of a tree made up of successively smaller sub-goals then the nearer the top of the tree the system operates the easier the system will be to use (see fig 3.2). If the system operates too far down the tree then the interaction will be constrained by the need for users to understand system 'primitives', how to string these together to meet sub-goals or plans, and how these combine to form the

A simple goal requires decomposing into
chunks the computer can handle:

Goal:
                        Calculate the mean

Split into:
                        Add the numbers
                        Divide sum by number of
                        numbers

Split again;
                        Add first to second
                        Add sum to third
                        Add sum to fourth
                        .....

Fig 3.2 Sub-dividing tasks

various plans which are required to meet the user's goal.
Clearly such an approach is undesirable if the system is to
become generally usable.

The problem in moving away from 'Computer Driven
Dialogue' is that the issues involved in good interface design
rapidly become complex, not for the user, but for the system
designer.

Computer driven dialogue is easy to implement; it requires
little or no understanding of the user or the task which the
system is required for. Indeed such knowledge might interfere
with the crude 'efficiency' of the machine, and such thinking
has been discouraged. It is a well known fact (sic) that users
are infinitely flexible and infinitely adaptable. This has been
proven many times by the sale and success of several
incredibly complex systems. It is not worth listing the large
number of word-processor packages which require their users
to adopt a range of thinking modes and models, none of which

bears any semblance to the basic task of inputting text. Fortunately this is ceasing to be the case.

The main market for computers used to lie in the computer industry, and users were computer professionals, practising a black Art. By contrast, today's larger markets for computer systems will be open to significant sales penetration only if the interfaces are easy to use for today's typical user - a non-specialist with no interest in penetrating the arcane delights of, for example, the Unix command language. Computer driven systems tend to alienate all but the expert or dedicated user. There is a requirement for systems not only to be useful but also to be usable. Developments in Artificial Intelligence, and in particular expert systems, in parallel with developments in cognitive psychology are starting to address these problems. The sale of 'user friendly' systems and software into mass markets has required many organisations to reconsider their design philosophy. Whereas functionality, functionality and functionality used to be enough, issues of usability are starting to assume a more prominent role.

Good design starts with the designer at the earliest stages of system development. To produce the usable, useful computer, the designer needs an intimate knowledge of who these users are and what their tasks will be. It is vital that designers have this understanding at the very beginning so that the system will embody some knowledge about both the task and the user, and hence achieve the user's goals.

3.4 SIMPLE MODELS OF THE USER

If the user can be clearly defined, the task concisely described, and the situation is unlikely to change with time, then the system is able to incorporate a 'static' model of the user and define the system interaction around that model.

Similarly, if several user groups can be distinctly defined, and each group occupies a distinct, discrete position on some scale, then a number of user models might be constructed and the system could incorporate several user-dependent modes of operation. This approach is analagous to Minsky's 'frames' approach to knowledge representation. Fig 3.3 illustrates the use of a frame based representation to describe different users as different specialisations of the breed. The models contained in the system can be used to support a higher level

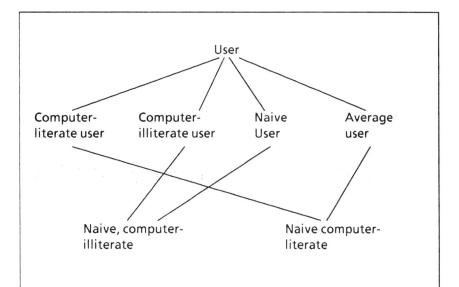

The frame-based representation is essentially an "is-a" hierarchy. Each frame in such a hierarchy can be viewed as a specialisation of each of its ancestors, and each link can be read as "is-a" moving up the tree. The representation is economic, because behaviour defined once for a general class towards the top of the tree can be inherited by each of its specialisations. As one moves down the tree, one can make local additions to create more specialised frames.

Fig 3.3   Frame hierarchies

of dialogue. If the system is able to embody knowledge about the user and the user's goals, then the system is able to translate the user's goals into its own representation and then construct its own sub-goals from underlying primitives which the user need not be aware of. Thus the system becomes easier to use, because the user is not required to map out every detail of an overall plan encompassing all the sub-goals.

For example, if the user wishes to calculate a mean, then the computer is requested simply to 'calculate the mean of 4, 3, 6, 5.4, ...'. The computer then interprets this request and calculates the mean. Whilst this is a simple example, the technique becomes of more use when the computer is able to supply an appropriate level of help or even deduce the error because it has an accurate model of the user's aims.

The idea of building discrete models of the user can easily be understood in the context of a simple example: multiple-level help systems. These multi-level help systems represented the first realisation by system designers that they were dealing with more than one type of person. The user of the system is able to specify the type of help required. For example, using the word processor package Wordstar, a user is able to choose from a four level help menu. The help level chosen is supposed to reflect the experience of the user and affects the information presented on the screen. This simple example has required the designer to construct 4 different models – even if the models are very crude – each model reflecting a different user, or category of user.

Such help systems are the first crude user models to have been developed. Such models are static and discrete, that is they do not change with time and are distinct from each other. They generally require users to categorise their own level of competence, along the lines of: 'Please type 1 if you are a naive user' etc. Furthermore, they do not serve to raise the level of abstraction away from that at which the system can work.

Another way in which the user is being considered and where the level of the dialogue is being raised is in the Fourth Generation Language (4GL) programs. These systems are supposed to be capable of generating code from high level input. Again, these are not ideal systems, but in order to make them work the designer has been required to make user models. Whether these are explicit or implicit, the models have enabled the systems to take high-level goal directed instructions and translate them into a much lower-level command language which the computer understands. 4GLs are able to automatically assemble primitives into plans to follow goals.

Yet another way in which systems are allowing for user modelling is by allowing the users to build their own models. These generally involve the user putting together commands and procedures into macros which can be called at another time, or defining abbreviations, which can be used as the individual's understanding of the system deepens.

The three examples above, whilst very different, do indicate a need for the user to be considered at the earliest of stages if the system is to be successful.

3.5 ADAPTIVE, STATIC USER MODELS

The next significant step in the development of user models is to make those models explicit and to require the system, rather than the user, to determine when a particular model applies. Such systems will contain several static models of the user (as described above). Each model characterises users in terms of performance using the system. Thus the system needs to carefully monitor the user's behaviour, and as that behaviour changes, employ the relevant model.

One often used idea is that of a user 'Agent': a front-end software layer supported by a relational database. The idea of this sort of Agent for enhancing interface design has been developed by Wilson et al. (3) in the form of an 'Active Mailbox'. Again the crucial feature of the system is that the user is not aware of the low level primitive interactions but is able to operate using high-level planning/goal directed behaviour.

For example, an Active Mailbox might incorporate an intelligent 'secretary'. This is a program which examines the destinations and senders of mail and classifies it according to some standard: for example, junk mail night be mail with multiple destinations, whilst urgent mail might come from the boss.

Both these systems do require some user awareness of the underlying system and are not truly automatic. Although the systems are significantly better than the simple multi-level help type systems described previously, the user still needs to perform crucial actions and make decisions which might be better left to the system. Ideally, the system should be capable of deciding on the user's type from information gathered.

An example of the development of such a system is the Adaptive Intelligent Dialogue System, which is being developed under the Alvey programme. This system contains a number of models of the user which are described in terms of the user's performance in system use. Users are moved from model to model as the system detects variations in their performance. Users are only aware of the transition from one model to the next by the changes in the screen held information or the level of help supplied when a problem is encountered.

The system decides when the user is becoming an expert by monitoring the type of commands input, the mistakes made and the understanding the user has of the system (as shown by the ability to perform operations correctly). The system has a number of rules which define what an expert's behaviour is, and these incoRporate factors such as the user of command abreviations, the use of the help facilities, the number and type of errors made, etc.

It is important to appreciate that this system operates by the application of knowledge at the design stage. Expert knowledge on the respective amounts of information required by naive and experienced users must be explicitly stated. Also, the user models must be defined in terms of explicit behaviour patterns which the system must build up and interpret from the only information available to it (ie the keystrokes input by the user).

The main problem with this type of system is that the models are discrete. The user is not viewed in terms of slowly altering over time, with some areas being well developed and others never used. This would require too many models to be stored. Instead, simpler, representational models are created. Whilst these are significantly better than previous attempts to solve the problem they are not ideal.

A flat, stereotypic model of the user will not help to distinguish the UNIX expert, (who is unaware of a particular class of commands but is otherwise a complete expert), from the naive user. Both may even make the same type of mistakes – though the expert will learn more from the errors. Both users might be classified under the same model, but the expert will have a deep understanding of the system and a very steep learning curve. Kiss (4) in an attempt to define how individuals differ, described system users as 'Agents' – where an Agent has attributes of intentionality, memory, learning ability, as well as multi-dimensional characterisitcs which do not map well onto a two-dimensional scale. (NB. An Agent in Kiss's sense is different from Miller's conception, described earlier).

The need to consider the user's characteristics as lying on a multi-dimensional continuum has led to the development of more sophisticated models, accounting for more complex behaviour. Such models must incorporate a far more complex and deeper understanding of the users, but should, perforce, produce a better system.

3.6 DYNAMIC MODELS

A dynamic, continuous user model does not categorise the user in terms of discrete models. It attempts to produce a multi-dimensional map with many different aspects, reflecting the myriad user types. Shackel (12) has described a few of the user types and attempted to identify the differences between classes such as the new user, the naive but frequent user, the skilled but infrequent user, the knowledgeable but inexperienced with this particular system user, and so on.

The problem is that even defining the user types is difficult. It is unclear how to elicit this information and even more difficult to build the information into a computer system. Building such a system would require the system designer to have a detailed knowledge of human behaviour, learning patterns, task requirements. Sometimes it is difficult for designers to produce systems which contain any models the user can relate to. Thimbleby notes (5):

> 'Interactive computer systems are much harder to use than we like to think. We expect, and often require, users of interactive computer systems to handle ontological problems that are comparable to mathematical problems which have defeated the best minds for millenia'

He further concludes:

> 'In general, computer systems do not operate with the same task models as their users. '

In other words, sometimes the designers not only fail to understand the user, they also fail to understand the problem. They build into the system assumptions which are false, and which, when the user explores such concepts, cause the system to either fail, or worse, produce an incorrect answer.

The deficiencies of the computer's task model can be traced back to the system designer, whose knowledge about humans and the problem which the system is solving is poor and incomplete.

A sophisticated interface must be capable of coping with these problems. It must be able to perform interactive planning, by allowing the user to input information, then provide guidance, help or advice where appropriate. It must be knowledgeable about the user's capabilities and characteristics. This knowledge should be built into the system, but the system must be able to modify it as the system gains more information about specific users. It must be capable of combining this knowledge with knowledge about the interface and the problem domain. The knowledge should be used to formulate goals and act on goals which the user is able to input directly. Indeed, the characteristic of any high-level system is that it is capable of determining goals and acting on them in a goal directed manner.

This implies that the designer must obtain this knowledge in the first place and emphasises the need for a design model which includes the user and the task.

It is interesting to note the recurrance of the the word 'knowledge'. Not surprisingly, most of the systems which do exhibit such behaviour are IKBSs of one kind or another.

It is worth speculating on the potential of a system which is capable of interacting at a high level with a user. One of the first disciplines to benefit from such a system would be knowledge engineering. Goals could be seen in terms of eliciting knowledge from the user or determining inconsistencies in a user's response. The system would endeavour to satisfy these goals by asking the user questions, without prompting or by some form of logic checking. Such systems might be less sophisticated than a 'complete solution' with the computer having a comprehensive model of the users, nevertheless the users would be modelled using several different factors with some fine tuning.

The task facing the designer of such systems is complex. High-level dialogue systems require sophisticated techniques to work well. Currently much work in AI is concentrating on addressing the question of representing the situations which form the contents of goals. Such work will be used to produce systems which will be able to 'understand' the nature of goals and to formulate methods of achieving them eg through the use of frames, scripts, semantic nets, etc. This work will produce systems which appear to exhibit goal directed behaviour provided that the user's model of the system matches the system's model of the user (see later).We can clearly see an overlap between IKBS and Human factors research in this area. At the same time that Human Factors specialists are recognising the importance of goal-directed problem solving techniques allied to explicit and separate knowledge of the user, IKBS specialists are using a similiar approach to building expert systems. The mapping is shown in fig 3.4. An expert system has a knowledge base containing knowledge, some of which is in use at any one time, and thus likely to be seen in the working memory (perhaps in a form slightly modified to take account of the current activity). The inference engine organises both this process and the input from the user to carry out processing. Similar comments apply to the advanced user interface.

Most commonly used expert system inference techniques are goal directed. For example , simple backward chaining rule-based systems (the *sine qua non* of the small shell world) can easily be viewed as decomposing a major goal into a number of sub-goals. An example is shown in fig 3.5.

However, the system is unable to distinguish between two equally valid solutions (valid in system terms). This can be a major problem with expert systems. The input can produce more than one valid solution, and often only the first solution which satisfies the conditions is produced. Even more importantly, the order in which the information is input can affect the solution produced. Thus, even when using declarative, rather than procedural, programming the solution can be determined by order.

A simple way to solve this problem is to produce another valid solution at the user's request, or to present a list of all valid solutions. This will not help the user choose. Indeed, in the user's terms only one solution will do. Unfortunately, the communication between the system and the user has not established this fact. The system has no understanding of the relative desirability of the different solutions. Thus, research is needed into the area of desirability. To solve this problem, the system must incorporate a deeper understanding of the

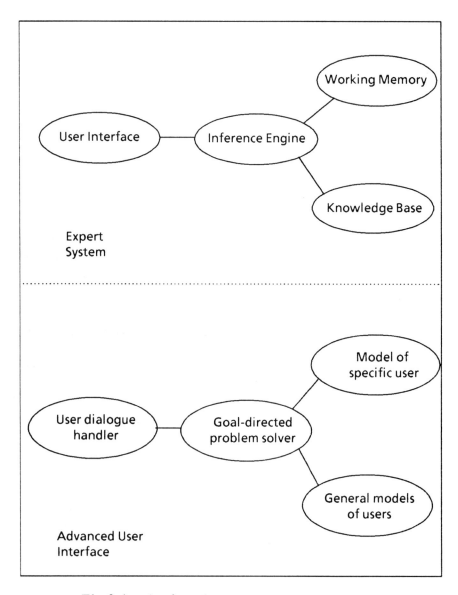

Fig 3.4   Analogy between an expert system
and an advanced user interface

user's needs and motivation to produce a solution which goes
beyond the criteria proposed explicitly by the user.

Given the goal, "decide what to wear" and this rule set:

if choice of trousers is made and choice of shirt is made
then decision about what to wear is made

if weather is sunny then wear t-shirt

if weather is cold then wear sweater

if job is messy and weather is cold then wear jeans

if job is not messy and weather is cold then wear smart trousers

if weather is warm then wear shorts

Then the overall goal can be broken down thus:

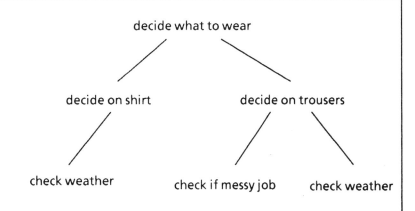

(It is also interesting to note that this goal hierarchy can be
entered at any point, dependent upon the scope of the
current task - a useful feature for any goal-directed system)

Fig 3.5   Backward chaining rules as a goal–directed
mechanism

It seems reasonable that in cases where more than one solution matches the user's goals, but the different solutions have differing levels of acceptability, to postulate a lack of understanding of the user's goals. Co-operative systems (see Chapter 5) make some attempt to alleviate this problem, by attempting to elicit some of the implicit assumptions that the user makes about the system. This approach may also help the user to build an accurate understanding of the system, by giving feedback to requests which make unreasonable assumptions about what is possible.

3.7 SUMMARY OF SYSTEM MODELS

We have considered three main axes for the system model; whether it is explicit or implicit, discrete or continuous, and dynamic or static. These models are shown in fig 3.6, which represents the range of models using a three dimensional graph. One can see eight separate areas emerging, each representing a different class of system. Whilst such a description is not complete, it does serve to illustrate the major divisions. It also emphasises the point that the distinctions between model types such as explicit or implicit are not hard and fast, but instead are somewhat blurred.

The next problem to consider is the ways in which the system's view of the user relate to the user's view of the system.

3.8 USER MODELS OF THE SYSTEM

When a system is designed employing knowledge about users and their goals new problems occur. We have so far concentrated on the system's model of the user. It is very important to remember that users also build their own internal models of the system. It is crucial that these models match. We have already noted the consequences of making the user think in an unnatural way. Whenever there is a mis-match, users will produce errors. The particular difficulty is that the errors will not 'make sense' to a user who is trying to understand the errors in the context of a mistaken view of 'what is really happening'.

Similar problems can occur when employing high level models of the user. If the user/system models do not match,

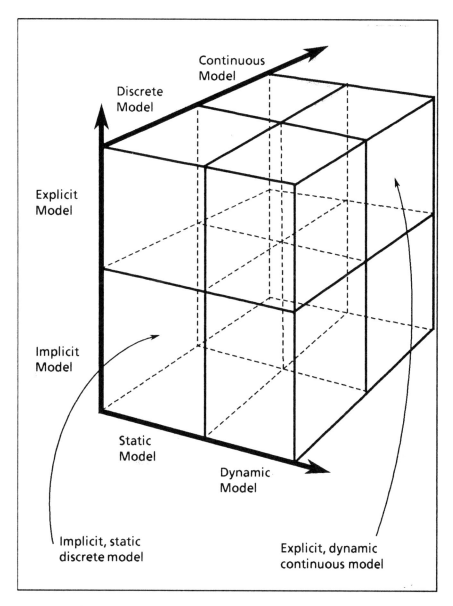

Fig 3.6 Graphical view of the different classes of system
models

then the user's performance can rapidly deteriorate.
Sometimes the system's operation will be opaque to the user.

For example, Suchman (6) studied users' performance on a photocopier which employed an intelligent help system. Whilst the system incorporated a detailed user model, the user was quite often unable to interpret the system's response. As an example, consider what happens when a photocopier senses that it is out of paper. It attempts to inform the user. The user misses the signal, and attempts to use the photocopier. The system realises the user's error and changes state, by which time the user has detected the problem and corrected it. Unfortunately the user is now faced with a new error which is based on the new state of missing the original error message. All very confusing!

The user interprets the system's response in terms of an internal model which has been built of how the system works. If this model is at odds with the way in which the system actually works or, as importantly, different from the internal model the system has of the user, then confusion occurs. The interaction suffers from 'cognitive dissonance' - there is a mis-match between the different ideas, models, plans and goals. The user's expectations of how the system should perform are at odds with its actual performance.

Another feature of user modelling is the effect the system has on users once they are aware of how the system operates and what sort of model the system has of them. This problem has lead to the development of systems which contain meta-models of the users' behaviour - plans about plans, the catering for the effect of the: 'I know that you know that I know' syndrome.

Such requirements illustrate a common problem with the design of dialogues and interfaces. No matter how sophisticated and complete the model is, there is always another layer. It appears that one can never determine all the factors which need to be included. This is likely to remain the case. Psychology has yet to fully understand the human mind and user modelling has limitations which stem directly from this.

The most important factor is the effect this incompleteness has on the interaction. If the model operates well enough without the full set of data then from a practical viewpoint the model is complete.

There are many potential benefits from systems which are able to employ high level dialogue design and exhibit goal directed behaviour. They generally do become more transparent and are usable by non-experts in computing. Such systems would be truly user-friendly, a term which has been so abused as to become almost meaningless when applied to describe most systems.

A user-friendly system would be capable of acting as an intelligent aid to a non-computer expert. It would be able to elicit knowledge from the user and incorporate that in an adaptive way to its model of the user. Currently knowledge elicitation is described as a major bottle-neck in the design of IKBSs. Experts require experts to elicit knowledge from them. This knowledge is then used to construct systems which are used to aid non-experts. If high level design principles could be formulated and applied then experts would be able to act as their own knowledge engineers (see Chapter 7).

A major stumbling block in this process is the lack of any underlying principles for what constitutes good Human-Computer Interaction, independently of any particular application. There is a need for the establishment of design criteria for HCI which are independent of the domain - the so-called domain independent HCI. An Alvey project is addressing this area and its conclusions should be used to ensure the better design of systems (see (2)).

3.9 USER MODELS OF THE SYSTEM - SOME THEORETICAL MODELS

We have described a number of system models of the user. It has already been stated that the interaction is a two-way process and we must consider the role the user plays.

The user's model of the system is of crucial importance if the system is to be successfully used. In all systems, irrespective of how they have been designed, it is the user who determines the system's success or failure. The most important fact to recognise is that people have many different models of systems. It will not suffice to consider one model which explains all computers. This is intuitively obvious, yet it is surprising how many systems are designed along the lines of 'if it worked last time for that application, it will work this time, for a completely different application.'

The next important fact is that the user's model is rarely static. The model will be redefined with exposure to the system. Two important phases can be recognised:

- The training phase - users' models will be defined in terms of how they are trained to use the system. Their understanding of what the system is, and what they believe the system is capable of, will be based on this training.

- The experienced user's model - once the system is used, experience alters the user's perception of the system, causing the model to be honed, redefined in the light of experience and modified to account for new features and new experiences.

It is important to note that the model formed during training will provide the user with a basic framework, which can remain largely unaltered, even in the light of conflicting evidence. The user may be convinced that the system operates one way, even when using it in another. This conceptual set is difficult to deal with. When the user's model is inaccurate, then even if the solution is 'obvious' or trivial, the user might be unable to resolve the problem.

Several types of models have been distinguished. Stevens and Collins (7) and Smith and Collins (8) highlighted a few. These are in many respects analogous to the models which the system contains of the user but reflect the user's understanding of the system, rather than the designer's understanding of the user. In all cases, it is the perceived characteristics of the system which determine the user's model, it is not the actual characteristics of the system.

Fig 3.7 illustrates one of the ways in which the user's view of a computer system can be decomposed. Even this relatively simple view shows that a user is operating on five distinct levels.

The levels shown in fig 3.7 are described in fig 3.8.

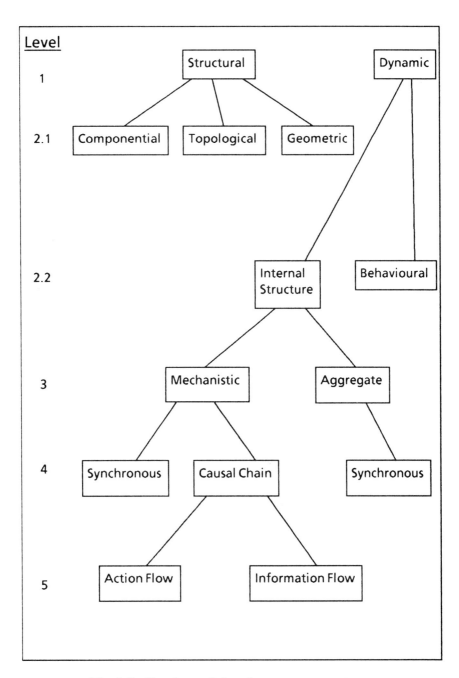

Fig 3.7 User's models of computer systems

Level	Description
1. Structural vs. dynamic	A structural model does not vary with time: a dynamic model does.
2.1 Componential vs. topological vs. geometric	A componential model comprises simply a number of defined components. A topological model specifies some connection (either spatial or conceptual) between the components. A geometric model specifies explicit spatial relationships.
2.2 Behavioural vs. internal structure	A behavioural model is made up of 'black boxes' with specified inputs and outputs, whereas the internal structure model attempts to account for the system in terms of the interactions between different sub-components.
3. Aggregate vs. mechanistic	Aggregate models assume that each component behaves in a uniform manner. Mechanistic models distinguish between components.
4. Synchronous vs. causal chain	Events can occur either simultaneously, or within some causal chain. (aggregate models are inherently synchronous).
5. Action flow vs. information flow	Some models assume that only information flows through the system, whereas others are based around the idea of some substance or energy flowing through the system.

Fig 3.8 Levels of user models of systems

Whilst these models do not serve to explain all user behaviour (nor are they an exhaustive list of the models users make) it is soon apparent that there are no simple, single models which can account for an individual's behaviour. Nor is it immediately apparent how to determine a particular user's model or models. Similarly, there is no reason to assume that a complex model formed by a user is self-consistent and logical in all respects. A further consideration is the 'grain' level of the user's model, that is , the level of detail of the user's model. Naturally, a coarse grained model is simpler, easier to understand and easier to act upon, whereas a fine grained model, whilst neccesary to understand some systems, will be much more difficult to cater for.

Work by Young (9 & 10) on the use of calculators illustrates the difficulties which occur when there is a mis-match between system and user models and also indicates what models should be used as a design guide.

Young found that a particular reverse Polish notation calculator was inherently difficult to use because it was based on a 'surrogate model'. This is a model which does not map between the task and the actions necessary to carry out the task. Thus, rather than inputting numbers which are to be added then divided by a third in the obvious way of 1 + 2 / 3, the user must input 1 + 2 / = 3 =, which, as Smith and Goodman state (11), 'is only obscurely related to the original [task]'. Thus it is the task-action mapping which is crucial and which should be used to guide good design.

3.10 HUMAN-CENTRED: AN APPROACH TO GOOD DESIGN

We have described the problems of not considering the users, and the problems when the user is considered. This section outlines some of the practical considerations which lead to good design and considers the design of expert systems. Shackel (12) outlines an anthropocentric approach to design, suggesting that the designer should consider the user at the centre of a bulls-eye and design accordingly (see figure 1.2). This approach is as valid for system design as for equipment design. The tools might be different, but the aim is the same, to build something which the end-user can use.

In the case of expert systems the most important features in the design process are the nature of the expert's knowledge and the user for whom the system is being built.

Step one in the design process is to elicit the user's needs, but in order to fully determine how the system can help, the process of acquiring the expert's knowledge must also begin. This can be done in a number of ways from informal discussions, through semi-structured interview to comprehensive task analysis (see Chapter 7). The unique aspect of expert systems is the nature of the information collected. The information gathered at this point in the design process will be incorporated into the system, which will be later used by the individual. Obviously the system might be used by people other than the supplier of the original information and more than one expert might be used as sources of basic information. However, a crucial feature of the expert system is that it relies on the expert, a non-computer specialist, to construct it.

The expert also acts as the main tester of the system. Once the knowledge is incorporated into the system, it is the expert who tests the knowledge and spots inconsistencies, inaccuracies and difficulties. At the same time, the user tests the system's interfaces. Obviously, expert and user may be one and the same person, and even if this is not the case it is likely that the expert will be required to use part of the system's interfaces (for example, to modify the system's knowledge at a later date).

This makes expert systems unique. This design approach is equivalent to designing a lathe by gathering information from expert woodworkers, building a lathe, whilst simultaneously modifying the prototype lathe in the light of comments from not only the expert woodworkers, but also less skilled workers who try the machine. The expert system builder's problems are exacerbated because lathe designers at least understand roughly what lathes and woodworkers are supposed to do.

Expert system design may need input from many sources. We have already introduced the problem of cognitive dissonance in the simple case where one human and one conventional computer program are interacting. The problems increase manyfold when one moves to an expert system where the number of interested parties increases. Fig 3.9 shows some of the interactions.

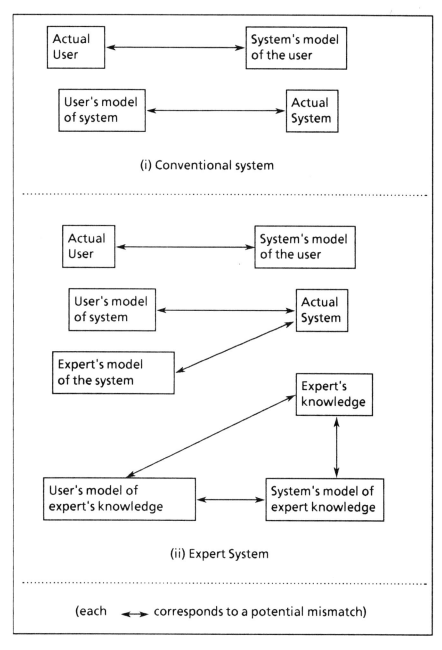

Fig 3.9   Sources of cognitive dissonance

In fact, if an expert system is to function effectively, the design of the system must be user-centred (refer to fig 1.2), and the actual system must reflect as closely as possible the way the expert tackles the problem. This is because the user's model will probably be coloured by the way he or she interacted with the human expert before the advent of the expert system (this last point only applies where user and expert are separate individuals, of course).

In theory, expert systems should be the best designed, most individually tailored systems available.

Problems arise in the same way that problems occurred when we moved from the craft-age to the machine-age. Commercially viable expert systems seek to aid the expert and the non-expert. It is rarely cost effective or sufficient to tailor one system to one user. The expert supplies the knowledge, this is interpreted by the knowledge engineer, the system is built, verified by the expert and released. It contains the expert's knowledge of the task, the expert's model, the knowledge engineer's interpretation and the modifications necessary to input the model into the system.

Ignoring the problems of resolving conflicting expert's views and assuming that a system can be built which satisfies the experts, we must consider the implications of the design on other users.

One of the main differences between experts and non-experts is their understanding of the problem. Their knowledge about solutions differs because of the vast array of heuristic, rule-of-thumb knowledge which the expert can bring to bear. As this knowledge is implicit, rather than explicit, it is implicit in the model. The knowledge engineer might be unaware of its existence. The manifestation of this is that the subgoals which make up a given overall goal are quite different for expert and end-user. A system can be designed along these lines which performs perfectly acceptably to the expert. It provides the information which the expert requires and represents some distillation of the expert's knowledge. When this system is used by naive or inexperienced users it inexplicably fails. Although the knowledge is there, it is not in a form which the new user can use.

Although the system has been designed by non-computer specialists with laymen in mind, the range of lay users is wider than that considered by the designers. The expert and the end-user are fundamentally different. They might become the same, in time, but simply considering the expert user when designing an expert system will not produce a system which is usable by non-experts wishing to obtain expert advice.

This consideration becomes paramount if we are considering designing expert systems for the general public. It is difficult to imagine a more tricky design problem. The person-in-the-street does not have well defined characteristics. The expert system cannot be successfully designed with a simple user model.

3.11 CONCLUSIONS

Although well designed computer systems have always required user models it is only by incorporating recent developments in AI that those models can now be built.

User models should not be seen in isolation. The human-computer interaction must contain an account of how the user sees the system. This view is often complex and at odds with the design.

The view is difficult to elicit and changing. It is likely to change most as the user learns how the system works. Once formed it will be less likely to radically change and may even remain fixed in spite of evidence that it is wrong.

A poor match between the user's model of the system and the system's model of the user will produce systems which are difficult to use . Also users will be more prone to produce errors from which they can not recover, as they lack the basic system understanding required to determine the correct response.

We have presented the two sides of the interface. The system should ideally cope with both models. It is at the interface that the two models meet (fig 3.10). Thus the considerations outlined in Chapter 2 apply and are defined by those outlined in this chapter.

In the next chapter we explore one particular interface type, natural language, in more detail. We hope to show that natural language has the potential to provide the most

Figure 3.10   User and system – who's modelling who?

appropriate input method to allow the reconciliation of the two sides of the interaction.

3.12 REFERENCES

1.   Parnas D, (1985) 'Software aspects of strategic defense systems,' University of Victoria, Dept. Computer Science

2. For further details on the Domain Independent Man-machine Interface project, contact the Alvey Directorate, Kingsgate House, 66-74 Victoria St, London SW1E 8SW

3. Wilson et al, (1984) 'The active mailbox - your on-line secretary,' IFIP Conference on computer-based message services, Nottingham University

4. Kiss G, (1983) 'Power vs. Generality - Theoretical constraints for HCI,' Proc. The User Interface; the ergonomics of interactive computing, The Ergonomics Society

5. Thimbleby H W, (1986) 'Ease of use - the ultimate deception,' Proc 2nd BCS-HCI Conference, British Informatics Society

6. Suchman L, (1985) 'Plans and situated actions,' Palo Alto: Xerox Corp

7. Stevens A L and Collins A, (1980) 'Multiple conceptual models of a complex system,' in Snow R, Federico P and Montague W (eds), 'Aptitude, learning and instruction; Cognitive process analysis,' Hillsdale, N J Erlbaum

8. Smith E E and Collins A, 'Applied cognitive psychology,' BBN Report #5499, Naval Research (code 458), NTIS document number AD-A136780

9. Young R M, (1981) 'The machine inside the machine: users' models of pocket calculators,' International Journal of Man-Machine studies, 1981, 15, 51-85

10. Young R M, (1983) 'Surrogates and mappings: two kinds of conceptual models for interactive devices,' in Gentner D and Stevens A L (eds), 'Mental Models,' Hillsdale NJ, Erlbaum

11. Smith E E and Goodman L, (1982) 'Understanding instructions: the role of explanatory material,' BBN Report #5088, Bolt Beranek and Newman Inc, Cambridge, Mass.

12. Shackel C J, (1974) 'Applied ergonomics handbook,'IPC Business Press Limited

4

Natural language

4.1 INTRODUCTION

This chapter addresses two different but related issues. The first issue is how to interpret natural language input to a computer. There are many approaches to this problem and these are highlighted here. Included in this chapter is a review of commercially available software.

There is then an examination of the issues for using natural language interfaces for expert systems.

4.2 TECHNIQUES FOR NATURAL LANGUAGE INTERPRETATION

Several techniques are available for interpreting natural language input to a computer. The objectives of all are broadly similar; to extract semantic meaning from human input. The approach used is dependent upon the parameters governing the particular interaction. A number of issues must be resolved before choosing an appropriate method. These include:

- Size of vocabulary.

- Use of non-grammatical input.

- The number of different users of the systems.

- Whether the principal user population is composed of regular or occasional users.

- The extent to which each individual sentence within a session will refer to others within that session.

- Whether the user population will mature with time.

4.2.1 Traditional approaches

The simplest approach to interpreting the meaning of natural language is to separate the analysis of syntax from the extraction of 'meaning'. It appears at first sight reasonable that all grammatical sentences can be divided up, or parsed, into a tree structure using certain rules describing what constitutes a well formed sentence. An example of this process is shown in fig 4.1.

The extraction of meaning (semantic analysis) then follows from the results of this syntactic analysis. The syntactic parse should indicate such features as whether the verb is passive or active, the subject or object of the sentence, and so on. The meaning can therefore be easily drawn out.

This process has the advantage of simplicity. Each of the phrase structure rules shown in fig 4.1 stands independently, and the grammar can easily be extended to handle further sentence types by the addition of more rules. The approach is well suited to simple sentences in tightly constrained domains. A user is able to build a comprehensive set of rules and ensure that these are followed. New words can be added and defined in terms which the system understands.

However, there are disadvantages with this. Firstly, a given sentence may be capable of being parsed in more than one way (two examples of this are shown in fig 4.2).

Secondly, it is not possible to handle ungrammatical text in this fashion. For example, consider this fragment of dialogue;

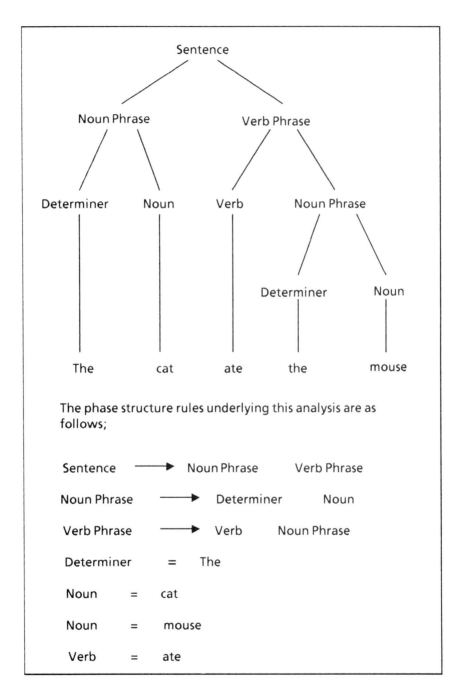

Fig 4.1 Parsing a sentence using simple phase structure rules

(i) The sentence

'The cottage I had built fell down.'

can be interpreted either as

'The cottage that was built by me fell down'

or as

'The cottage whose construction I had instigated fell down'

The correct meaning can be distinguished only by turning to a previous reference to the cottage, or by knowledge of the speaker (eg. Did she/he have either the skills or the time to build a cottage ?)

(ii) The sentence

'Johnny hit all his brothers with a bat'

leaves several questions, such as

'Did he hit them all with one blow ?'
'Did he hit them all with the same bat ?'
'Did he throw the bat at them ?'
'Was the bat of the cricketing or flying variety ?'

Some of these questions can be answered with general knowledge about the world. Also, some might not matter.

Fig 4.2 Parsing Problems

User: Please give me a list of all the customers who bought meat pies last week.

Computer: Mr. Smith, Mr. Jones

User: The week before ?

Computer: Mr. Jones

The user's second question is clearly ungrammatical, and yet is typical of interactions between humans. This particular type of ungrammatical back reference is known as ellipsis.

Thirdly, certain sentence types, whilst grammatical, pose problems. An example is conjunction. This occurs with sentences such as;

Harold saw a sovereign and picked it up.

It is virtually impossible to devise a set of simple phrase structure rules which can always identify what the 'it' of this sentence refers to.

In order to distinguish between alternative parses of the same sentence, humans often resort to either knowledge about the 'real world,' or possibly their recollections of earlier stages in the dialogue. Using knowledge of the 'real world' is the equivalent to building a domain dependent system which employs heuristic processes, as well as simple syntactic and semantic analyses. Similarly, using information gathered in earlier stages corresponds, in computer terms, to combining the syntactic and semantic analyses mentioned earlier. Much research is currently being directed at pursuing this two pronged approach.

Unfortunately there are difficulties with this combined approach. Hence several different extensions to pure syntactic analysis have been developed.

4.2.2 Transition networks

The problems mentioned above led to the development of Transition Networks. These operate essentially by working through a sentence from left to right. For each word, there are only a limited number of words which can grammatically follow it (given a structured, grammatical input). For example, the adjective big is only likely to be followed by another adjective, or by a noun (eg. 'big bus' and 'big red bus'). One can thus collect the noun and verb phrases encountered in fig 4.1. Each of the phrase structure rules of fig 4.1 can be rewritten as the route from the beginning to the end of a grammatical item. The network which the possible routes from a given startpoint to a completed noun or verb phrase form are described as a transition network.

Within the network, this information is represented by assigning nodes to 'states', and providing links between nodes which enable one to 'transform' from one state to another. Thus each link between nodes, or 'arc', represents a particular type of word, or perhaps another network defined elsewhere. Fig 4.3 defines the transition networks for the three rules of fig 4.1.

This approach does not confer any advantages of itself. Indeed, it is necessary to extend it to include a recursive facility (see below) in order to attain the same level of formal power as the simple phrase structure rules. However, a relatively straightforward set of enhancements can generate a significant increase in performance.

4.2.3 Augmented transition networks

The simple network is inadequate. Extensions are generally made in order to increase the generality of the system. A recursive facility enables the system to handle subordinate phrases. Also useful are registers which can be used to record information obtained in the analysis of one phrase which can affect other phrases. Thus, information such as singular/plural is noted, as are current candidates for major features of the overall sentence, such as subject. Other additions include rules which define when and how to modify the contents of the registers. Such an enhanced system is known as an Augmented Transition Network (ATN). An overall view is provided in (4).

4.2.4 Chart parsing

In contrast to the previously described techniques, which start from some concept of a sentence's overall structure and work down (a top-down approach), chart parsing is an approach

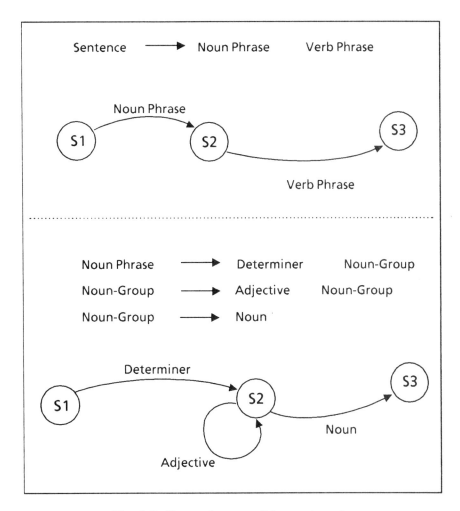

Fig 4.3 Example transition networks

which facilitates the building up of structure from small blocks (a bottom–up approach). The disadvantage of the top–down approach is that it can be very time consuming if an erroneous assumption is made early in the parsing process .

A second advantage of the chart parsing approach is that it may allow the extraction of some information from ungrammatical input.

There is, however, a major efficiency problem. A large number of irrelevant 'building blocks' may be created. Because of this problem, chart parsing is generally used only in conjunction with some other approach to syntactic parsing. See (5) for more details.

4.2.5 Case grammar

This technique represents a departure from what has gone before, in that some semantic information is used. In order to best understand the benefits conferred by case grammars, it is instructive to consider some of the limitations of the ATN approach described earlier. The use of registers can often enable an ATN to provide identical parses for sentences with the same meaning. For example, the similarity between the following pair of sentences can easily be spotted;

Harold gave James the salt.
Harold gave the salt to James.

However, matching a pair such as

An elephant's trunk picks things up.
Things can be picked up by an elephant using its trunk.

is beyond the ATN.

Similarly, sentences of virtually identical structure can often have very different meanings. Consider the following;

Jan works with tools.
Jan works with colleagues.
Jan works with ease.
Jan works with dolphins.

The Case Grammar ideas spring from the view of a sentence as a description of some underlying event. Hence associated with a given verb, one can describe a case-frame which has several slots, or cases. Each case specifies a participant in the event. So, for example, the verb 'go' will have a compulsory 'Actor' case to indicate who or what is going, and further optional cases to indicate where the Actor is going to, or perhaps, what colour the Actor is going.

An interesting side of Case Grammars is the ease with which they can be put to work in constructing output text.

An example of parsing using a Case Grammar is shown in fig 4.4.

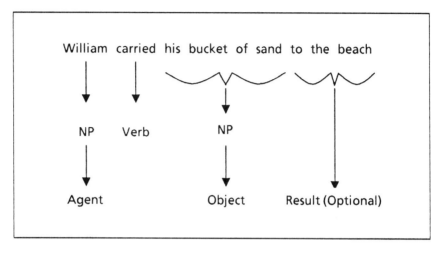

Fig 4.4 Case Grammar

4.3 CURRENT RESEARCH

The preceding section describes most of the techniques that have been used in current commercially available products. However, research into the problem of natural language interpretation is starting to indicate other solutions to the basic problem. This section provides an overview of recent developments. The object of this is to give some indication of the advances that can be expected from new products over the next few years.

4.3.1 Generalised phrase structure grammar

Generalised Phrase Structure Grammar (GPSG) is a technique which springs from earlier theoretical work in transformation grammars. That work has not been described in this book, essentially because although of great importance in the development of natural language parsing, it has not been used to any great practical effect. However, the underlying principle of transformation grammars is that two equivalent sentences can be identified by using certain well-defined transformations to map one on to the other.

As the work on transformation grammars continued, several extensions were found to be necessary to increase the generality of the parsers constructed. After some time, researchers such as Gazdar (1) noted that such extensions had largely removed the original need for transformations.

Instead, features and metarules were used. Features are items such as singular/plural for simple nouns, and other more complex properties for grammatical entities higher up the parse structure. They can be used to detect inconsistencies in parses which could otherwise be overlooked.

Metarules are rules which can be applied to other rules to enable the development of further rules.

The upshot is a syntactic grammar which uses simple structure (and hence is easily and efficiently parsed on a computer) but has extensions which provide significant power.

Hewlett-Packard Research Labs are currently working towards a commercially available product which should be available by end-1987.

4.3.2 Lexical functional grammar

Lexical Functional Grammar is another grammar likely to be seen in commercial use. It is currently undergoing development at Xerox PARC (where it was invented) and ICOT.

Lexical Functional Grammar is based on a very large lexicon where different forms of sentence parts such as verbs are stored. Alongside each of the stored entries is information about how to interpret related noun phrases. Its strength is the clearly defined functional structure, which provides an easy link to semantic interpretation.

4.3.3 Other grammars

Many other grammars are currently being developed, but none seems as close to becoming commercial products as GPSG and Lexical Functional Grammar.

Another problem which is being researched is that of

interpreting semantics. As yet the research is not sufficiently advanced to lead to commercial products and it seems likely that no advanced product will be produced in the short term. This is a key observation: the onus is on the system builder to handle the semantics, and to limit the grammar to avoid certain types of confusion.

4.4 THE PRODUCTS

The following is not intended to be in any way exhaustive, but to indicate a few examples of practical embodiments of the techniques described earlier. For a fuller list, see (7).

4.4.1 Intellect

Easily the most established product is 'Intellect,' produced by the Artificial Intelligence Corporation. It is marketed, and used, purely as an intelligent front-end to IBM and DEC application packages. It requires the user to develop his or her own lexicon.

The theoretical basis of Intellect is the use of ATNs, as described earlier. The system has now been available for five years and has been continually developed over that time, so that the emphasis should be very much upon the 'A' of ATN.

Intellect is very much a mainframe product, and its pricing reflects this. However, this is changing as AI Corporation are starting to look towards the PC market. The first step in this direction has been a version of Intellect for the DEC MicroVax.

Intellect is capable of interpreting fragments of well-formed sentences, such as the meat pie example in section 4.2.1.

4.4.2 Ramis II English

Competitors to Intellect include Ramis II English, produced by Mathematica Incorporated. Johnson (1985) describes this product as 'somewhat more robust and flexible than Intellect,' and notes that 'If Mathematica ... produces a more general purpose interface, Intellect's position as the market leader could be threatened' (7).

4.4.3 Language Craft

Produced by the Carnegie Group, this product has only recently been launched. It has been commercially available since 1985, subsumes the 'Plume' system, developed at Carnegie-Mellon University. It is claimed to be the first commercially available tool using a case-frame approach. Carnegie Group have also extended the basic concepts in a number of directions. This enables the system to handle a number of clause types, moving well beyond the most usual declarative and imperative sentence types.

This system is of special interest to AI Programmers, as it is produced in Common Lisp and is therefore likely to become available for a number of AI application machines. The system is already available on both Symbolics and DEC Vax.

Language Craft has three main modules, one which fills in case frames (see earlier), one which handles exceptional conditions, and finally a translator to generate output commands. The system will not handle relative clauses.

The system does seem to represent a significant development.

4.4.4 Menu-driven systems – NaturalLink

NaturalLink is a microcomputer-based product, produced by Texas Instruments. Although it is a natural language interface in some respects, the system is not as advanced as, say, Language Craft.

The basis of the interaction is that the user constructs pseudo-natural sentences from several menus. This obviously makes the parsing process much easier, as the number of possible user commands is finite, and ungrammatical input can be forestalled. This approach effectively overcomes all the problems of bounding the domain within which the user is allowed to work. Such a system does have merits. For example, the capabilities of the system are very clearly indicated to the user by the extent of the menu presented at each stage of the sentence construction.

The menu-driven approach is likely to be adequate for a range of applications. It does not allow the user the same freedom of expression as free-form input, but this will not be a problem in many cases (for example, an expert system which deals with a tightly constrained domain). Indeed, it seems reasonable that for most types of expert system such an interface could be constructed; the developer should carefully consider whether the extra effort in developing a full natural language interface is worthwhile.

The menu-driven approach may actually be superior in certain areas. For example, several expert systems allow the user to amend or add to the system's knowledge base. The use of a menu-driven system for the construction of if-then rules, for example, ensures that:

(i)   the logical structure of any rules constructed can be handled by the system
(ii) the user does not have to remember a multitude of special words, both system commands and the identifiers used to represent items described in the system knowledge base
(iii) the system is more accesible to the non-typist. In fact, for the fluent typist, the system may become slightly frustrating as familiarity grows.

Such systems have been used succesfully; apart from the TI product, one such has been developed as part of an interface to knowledge about causal links within a large process plant.

4.4.5 Talkwriters

The most sophisticated natural language products would be those which rely solely upon voice input. As yet, none are available. Several companies are planning to produce large vocabulary voice recognition systems in 1987/88, primarily in the talkwriter area. The degree to which such products will incorporate natural language understanding is not yet clear.

There are a number of other products on the market, but those described above should give a flavour. Perhaps the most important conclusion to note is the size of the gap between the technology being researched and the technology incorporated in current products. It seems inevitable that the next few years will see substantial improvements, including particularly the introduction of genuinely useful talkwriters.

4.5 APPLICATION AREAS

There are a number of application areas where natural language interfaces are useful. These include word processing (talkwriters and handwriting interpreters), database inquiry systems, context scanning and expert systems. Before moving on to consider in detail the application to expert systems, it is useful to briefly investigate progress in the other application areas mentioned.

4.5.1 Database Inquiry Systems

This is the most mature application area. As described above, mainframe products such as Intellect are targetted virtually exclusively in this area. Most such systems are relatively simple, and succeed by focusing on a fairly narrow domain. The users of such systems are generally professional personnel, and it is therefore quite acceptable for the system to either request clarification of difficult input or to be limited to certain sentence types. Perhaps the most interesting problem encountered in this area has been the tendency for users of such systems to develop unrealistically high expectations of the system's power. As will be discussed later, this is also a problem for expert system developers.

Relevant work includes Query by Example and Object by Example - both developed by IBM - and several systems built using Intellect. (2) provides an account of one such system.

4.5.2 Word processing ('TalkWriters')

Research programmes under Alvey are actively looking at the role which natural language interpretation can play to aid in speech recognition. Similar activities are being carried out in the US under the aegis of the SSI. It is not unreasonable to suppose that sentence information can be used to improve significantly the performance of speech recognisers. Most of the newer systems include some language model, either explicitly - with the user required to define allowable words in terms of the model - or implicitly, with the system determining its own rules from word useage. The main problem with incorporating language models is that they are language or even dialect specific. This problem aside, natural language rules are likely to provide a very powerful tool for increasing vocabulary sizes and accuracy.

4.5.3 Content scanning

Much research has gone on in this area. The aim of content scanning is to scan a stream of natural language text, such as Reuters' news service, for items of interest. The first commercial example of such a system, ATRANS, was announced by Cognitive Systems in 1985. This is aimed at the banking community.

Such systems are of interest because the definition of 'interest' is amenable to some form of knowledge-based system. The large domain which news streams typically address need not be an insurmountable barrier to producing usable systems in the near future. A 'bottom-up' approach to partial parsing, such as the chart parsing described earlier, will enable a system to identify and parse items of interest from within an otherwise incomprehensible stream of language. For the interested reader, (3) describes a good example of a content scanning system.

One interesting feature of content scanners in, say banking applications, is that they can be run in parallel with existing systems. This will provide important data on cost justification and the real use of such systems.

Owing to their simplicity (in application terms) it may be that content scanning systems will make the sort of breakthrough on the 1980s which XCON and Prospector made in the 1970s.

4.5.4 Other applications

Other applications include a front-end for the notoriously difficult to master Unix operating system (11), and also field of machine translation. This field is still in its infancy; (8) describes this area in more detail.

4.6 NATURAL LANGUAGE INTERFACES FOR EXPERT SYSTEMS

4.6.1 Naturalness

There are many arguments for providing a natural language front-end to an expert system. One of the most common reasons is to provide 'naturalness.' A justification might run something along the lines of: an expert system is supposed to behave like a human expert: its potential users are experienced at communicating with human experts by means of natural language: therefore a natural language interface will require minimal adaptation on the part of users.

In other words, a good natural language front-end will map well onto the user's model, and minimise dissonance between man and machine.

An immediate problem with this idea is that an expert system does not generally have the same breadth of knowledge and abilities as its human counterpart. Consider one of the best known expert systems, Mycin. Mycin can diagnose which blood disease a patient has with a degree of certainty comparable to the best consultants. However, the system would not be able to cope with a request for, say, the names of the three most commonly occurring diseases. Faced with an open natural language interface, there is a tendency for the user to overlook such limitations. A classic case of users anthropomorphising a system which provided a natural language interface but in fact employed simplified context spotting was ELIZA (see Chapter 1). The tendency of users to assign too high a level of intelligence to a system and thus encounter difficulties which would never have occurred to the system's builders is a recurrent problem. It appears people are all too willing to ascribe actions and motives to a computer, which merely reflects their view of the world. A good natural language interface is only likely to aggravate the problem.

This over-estimation of a system's scope will at the least lead to wasted time, and may ultimately have more serious consequences - a system can be rejected for failing to support facilities that a user might never have expected from a more conventional interface. The more complex the expert system, the greater this danger.

4.6.2 Comprehensibility

A natural language interface can also provide greater
comprehensibility. The ability of an expert system to provide
an explanation is regarded as one of the strengths of such
systems. Unfortunately, such explanations are often little more
than useless when provided as canned text joined by keywords.
If the text can be generated at runtime to suit the particular
query, then it becomes possible to provide different types of
explanation (see Chapter 6).

4.6.3 Cost

A full natural language interface will undoubtedly be
expensive. As mentioned earlier, menu-driven alternatives may
actually provide a better alternative, and will certainly bear a
lower construction cost. As yet no natural language system has
been a massive commercial success, comparable with, say,
Visi-Calc.

4.6.4 Current state of the technology

The earlier discussion of the technology has shown that the
powers of current commercially available systems are limited
to well-defined domains. Certain sentence types cannot be
handled, resolution of ambiguities is not well-handled and
ungrammatical input may not be fully understood. This is
largely due to the current emphasis on syntactic parsing.

The discussion of more advanced research has shown that
more powerful and general systems are on the way, and this
should be borne in mind for long-term developments.

4.7 SUMMARY OF NATURAL LANGUAGE INTERFACE DESIGN CONSIDERATIONS

In the preceding sections, the state of the art in natural
language systems has been described. This section addresses
the question of when natural language interfaces should be
used.

Natural language interfaces using commercially available
tools are not sufficiently robust for   occasional or non-

professional users. They should only be considered where the domain of discourse is limited.

Natural language may well be worth considering when constructing systems required to provide substantial amounts of explanation to the user.

The construction of more sophisticated systems from scratch is a major undertaking, and requires substantial research. For example, talkwriter projects both in the UK and US are forced to devote a lot of resources to produce even first generation systems.

A system which constructs pseudo-natural language from menus has some real advantages and may offer an acceptable low-cost alternative.

Fig 4.5 indicates the properties of an IKBS which will affect the suitability of a natural language interface.

4.8 MORE ADVANCED INTERFACE TYPES

The foregoing has made the tacit assumption that the natural language interface has functioned as a separate entity in front of a black box expert system. Thus the natural language interface has taken user input, parsed it to generate instructions for the expert system, and passed these on without extra information.

Several authors (notably Sparck-Jones (9)) have suggested that the real promise of natural language interfaces is to facilitate the construction of entirely new types of system. There are two major issues here, both of which have been discussed at length in the previous chapter: user modelling and dialogue control.

The main problem of dynamic user modelling systems, it will be recalled, is to construct a model or models of the user during the course of his or her interaction with a computer system. There are several types of model that may be generated. These attempt to describe, amongst other characteristics:

(i) the user's plan (underlying a sequence of commands)
(ii) the user's mental properties (How well does s/he understand

For	Against
A precisely defined domain	A loosely defined domain
A wide range of possible commands or system actions	When all interactions with the system are likely to follow one of a small range of options
When complex explanations are required	
	When the flexibility of natural language may lead the user into a false estimate of the system's capabilities
	When natural language may require the user to memorise many specialised words (and a menu-driven system may be better)
When a less familiar mode of interaction is likely to be rejected	When users are occasional or non-professional
When natural language may provide useful input to a user model	
When the system will be required to enter into a lengthy, mixed initiative dialogue	

Fig 4.5 Factors for and against using a natural language
interface for an IKBS

the domain of interest ? Is s/he computer literate ?)
(iii) the user's cultural background (see fig 4.6)

Sparck-Jones [9] has argued that the information necessary
to construct these models can only realistically come from the

more expressive natural language interface. It is also important to see that as the user modelling data are to be used by the expert system, then the natural language component of the system must become an integral part of the expert system, rather than remaining a loosely coupled front-end.

An example of the collection and later use of such data , by means of a better integrated natural language interface, is shown in fig 4.6 (taken from (6)).

$$\left.\begin{cases} \text{Do you have} \\ \text{Have you got} \\ \text{Have you} \end{cases}\right\} \quad \text{a Mrs Warwick in your passenger list ?}$$

The use of 'Do you have ... ' suggests an American speaker
The use of 'Have you ... ' suggests a conservative Englishman

Later, when the speaker states;

'It was important that she took the flight at 9am.'

the system can infer that Mrs Warwick **did** actually catch her flight when the speaker is American, but cannot make the same inference for the conservative Englishman. The cultural model of the user built up in the early part of the interaction has helped to resolve ambiguity at a later stage.

Fig 4.6. User modelling with natural language (taken from (6))

One of the fruits of recent human factors research has been an appreciation of the benefits of a mixed initiative dialogue. This implies that user and system are equally responsible for driving their dialogue, rather than, as is typical of most current computer systems, the computer taking most of the initiative.

This means that the user will often provide fairly lengthy and uninterrupted input, with the content unknown to the system in advance. The dialogue may continue between user and system at some length, with both sides introducing new concepts. Such a dialogue requires a highly flexible medium of exchange, and any artificial language with a similar degree of flexibility to the user's tongue is likely to be too complex for the user to learn.

4.9 CONCLUSIONS

Natural language understanding offers one way of facilitating good interface design. It is a complex issue. The benefits of natural language, in isolation, are still subject to debate. It is definitely the case that natural language does not preclude other user/system issues. Perhaps it is most interesting to explore the issues of natural language in relation to some particular application.

The next chapter continues on the interface theme, but adopts a more general perspective, covering the whole range of front end systems built using IKBS techniques.

4.10 REFERENCES

1. Gazdar, Klein, Pullum and Sag, 'Generalised Phrase Structure Grammar', Basil Blackwell

2. Waltz, D., (1976) 'Natural Language access to a large database: an engineering approach,' Proc. of 4th IJCAI

3. Marsh E., (1984) Hamburger H. and Grisham R., 'A production rule system for message summarisation,' Proc. AAAI 1984

4. Bates, M., (1978) 'The theory and practise of augmented transition network grammars,' Springer-Verlag

5. Kay, M., (1980) 'Algorithm Schemata and Data structures in syntactic processing,' Report CSL-80-12, Xerox PARC

6. Kilbury J., (1986) 'Language variation, parsing, and the

modelling of users' language varieties,' Proc. of 7th ECAI

7. Johnson, T., (1985) 'Natural Language Computing: the commercial applications,' Ovum Press

8. Hutchins, W.J., 'Machine Translation: Past Present & Future,' Ellis Horwood

9. Sparck-Jones, K., (1984) 'Natural language interfaces for expert systems,' Proc. of 4th conference of BCS Expert System SIG

5

Intelligent front-end processors

5.1 INTRODUCTION

This chapter describes intelligent front-end processors (IFEs). An intelligent front-end is software which sits between a user and a conventional software package. An IFE uses artificial intelligence techniques to enable the user to make more effective use of software packages.

The first part of this chapter describes a generalised IFE. Particular attention is paid to some of the theoretical issues governing areas such as dialogue control. This is followed by discussions of specific issues relating to some application areas. As far as possible, these are carried out within the context of the general framework described earlier. Finally, three practical systems are described.

5.2 FIRST PRINCIPLES

A typical IFE needs to accomplish a number of tasks. These are to:

- Carry out a dialogue with the user

- Produce a specification of the user's task or problem

- Use this specification to generate instructions for running a software package

- Interpret the results of running the package in the light of the user's specified problem(s)

- Relay answers to the user as part of the continuing dialogue

It is important to make two points. Firstly , the dialogue presented to the user will often be interactive. In other words, the results from one run of the target package will often form the starting point for the next set of instructions.

Secondly, the IFE may use a variety of techniques and aids, particularly when carrying out the dialogue with the user and producing the specification of the user's problem. The nature of the dialogue, for example, may often necessitate the use of a natural language interface. As described in the previous chapter, a natural language interface may often aid in the construction and maintenance of a model of the user (user modelling is discussed in more detail in Chapter 3). This model can then be used in resolving any ambiguities which occur in the user's aspirations.

Apart from maintaining a model of the user, and a specification (or model) of the task, some systems represent the package which is being front-ended by means of a third model.

5.3 THE DIALOGUE

The objective of the dialogue is to gain an understanding of the user's requirements. Bundy (1) has made a clear distinction between the control of the overall structure of the dialogue, and the detail of the method of the interaction.Particular devices used for the interaction will not be described here – Chapter 2 has presented the range available.

The aim of the dialogue ('to gain an understanding of the

user's requirements') is actually very broad. Ramsay (10) has
identified four more specific aims;

- Establishing the user's goals

- Obtaining more information about the task from
  the user

- Allowing the user to browse the system's
  knowledge about how to achieve those goals

- Answering user requests for explanation of the
  system's actions and conclusions

The first two of these can be carried out by a reasonably
traditional question and answer dialogue. The third is of
particular interest: the section covering IFEs for databases
later in this chapter is of relevance here. The fourth goal, to
provide explanations, is a fairly standard expert system
technique which is covered in Chapter 6.

Control of the overall structure of dialogue is an issue
often overlooked in systems of all types. Several IFEs are
reminiscent of simple rule-based expert system shells in this
respect – the dialogue is wholly machine-driven, with the user's
role reduced to answering questions when, and only when, the
system requires external input to its predetermined problem
solving strategy. This approach can be successful with a system
which operates within a tightly constrained domain, ie where
the tasks which the system addresses do not vary significantly
from one occasion to the next. Indeed, where adequate, such a
dialogue may well be preferable. It will certainly ease the
task of the system developer.

Unfortunately, IFEs because of their very nature tend only
to be applied to software packages which can be used to
perform a wide range of possible tasks.Furthermore, they are
often employed in situations where the user intentions are
unpredictable. Thus a dialogue driven by the system may well
prove inadequate. Alternative dialogues which are not system
driven can be either user–driven (see ECO below), or employ a
mixed-initiative dialogue, with the user and the system as
more or less equal partners.

A good example of a user–driven system is ECO (2). ECO is
a system which helps ecologists to build Fortran simulations.

This is achieved through users describing their views of a problem in something akin to natural language. (ECO is described in more detail later in this chapter.) An example of a system which operates a mixed-initiative dialogue is one constructed as part of an Alvey project. A collaboration in which the principals are International Computers Ltd (ICL) and the Department of Health and Social Security (DHSS) has carried out a large quantity of IKBS work within the 'DHSS Demonstrator Project.' One of the first fruits of this has been the 'Forms Helper' (14). The objective of this is to help DHSS claims clerks search a database of case precedents. The approach used is an iterative one. First the user partly fills in a form, and then criticises the system's attempts to find precedents which are similar in important respects. This critique drives the system's next attempt to meet the user's requirements, and the process is repeated until the user is satisfied. Thus user and system cooperate in the process of gradually refining the form against which precedents are matched, until a suitable set has been generated.

Further complications are introduced by the level of the user's experience. Ideally, the system will assume more of the initiative when faced with a novice user. The system should maintain a number of user models which can be used both to assess the user's 'type' and then to determine the interaction.

5.4 OTHER CONSIDERATIONS IN DIALOGUE DESIGN

The problem of controlling dialogue is one that extends beyond the confines of the IFE field. In particular, the importance of separating dialogue and task has become accepted by several workers. It is therefore of value to consider some of the problems of dialogue control in more depth.

5.4.1 Adaptation

Systems are designed to model the user, and to adapt their behaviour to suit that user. Unfortunately, users also adapt: they will modify their behaviour according to the system's responses and to their changing model or understanding of the underlying operation of the system. Without care, one will find a continuing mismatch, as both system and user continually adapt to each other's behaviour of a short time previously. The two will 'hunt' continually, rather in the way that some instruments do in standard control theory. The problem sounds rather theoretical: the practical effects are suprisingly widespread and make a major impact on the performance of systems and their users (see Chapter 3).

5.4.2 Representation

It is important to be able to represent the control of dialogue schematically. The two most commonly used approaches to dialogue control are transition networks and production rules. Essentially transition networks represent the space of possible dialogues as a network. Each node represents a question and answer, and the route through the network is controlled by the answer received from the user at each node. Such networks can be analysed by means of graph theory, and provided that the network does not grow to an embarrasingly large size, can provide an easy to understand overview of the dialogue . An example network is shown in fig 5.1.

If-then rule systems can be considered as dynamically generating such networks, or, more precisely, parts of such networks. These systems can have greater complexity (there is no need to represent the network explicitly, and so it can become arbitrarily complex) but are not amenable to rigorous analysis (the full network is not represented explicitly !).

We have touched on the concept of 'analysing' transition networks. Looking at fig 5.1, it is clear that some undesirable items can be identified by inspection - for example, unbreakable loops. Furthermore, the graphical representation makes it easy to avoid oversights in the dialogue design process. We can, where necessary, use a hierarchy of networks for design of large multifunctional systems. In such a situation, a complex decision might be represented as one node in a top level network, but be expanded into a network in its own right at a lower level.

However, such informal inspection is not the limit of the power of such networks. Formal methods are available for analysing such networks. These techniques can provide much information of use to the dialogue designer, the value of which is enhanced because its accuracy is guaranteed. One such formal technique is the use of 'path algebras'.

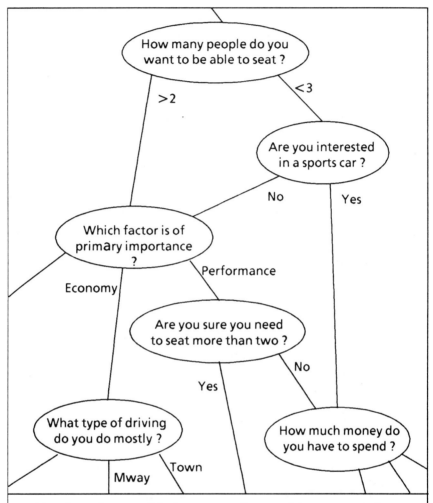

The above is a possible fragment of a transition network for a system designed to aid the user in the choice of a motor vehicle. One could construct such a network for any menu-driven system. However, such menu-driven systems are generally arranged in such a way that there are no links between different branches of the same node. The use of network representations makes it possible for the system builder to arrange things in a more complex fashion, without the danger that things will become too complex to understand.

Fig 5.1 Sample transition network

The technique is described by Alty (11) and an example of its use is given in (12). The details of the technique are not of importance to this discussion. Essentially, one proceeds by first labelling each arc within a network. Operators are then defined which can generate composite labels for sequences of arcs. Using this formalism, one can produce an 'adjacency matrix' which describes the links between nodes. It is also possible to generate higher order adjacency matrices, which provide information about paths of different types within the network.

The importance of this is that it enables the identification of useful subnets, and loops, and one can carry out functions which help with the checking of specifications.

CONNECT, a system described by Alty in (12), uses a production rule system to amend a transition network. The idea underlying this approach is to gain the theoretical power of analysis of networks, whilst retaining the flexibility of the rule-based approach. Only certain changes to the network are allowed: specifically, pre-defined arcs may be opened and closed. These 'switches' divide up the main network into sub-networks. The system is thus able to adapt to different levels of user performance. As the user performance changes in a certain way, a production rule fires. This either opens or closes an arc within the transition network, thus altering the sequence of questions which the system poses to the user in a given area of the dialogue.

This approach is attractive: we have earlier discussed the value of user modelling. The particular benefit of this approach is the explicit representation (through the current state of the network) of the system's model of the user. Because the system is represented as a transition network, it has been possible to make use of path algebras in identifying sub-networks, and greatly easing the complex task of checking that the network will 'work' properly.

5.4.3 Design by users

One approach to dialogue design is to let users design their own. Bateman (13) constructed the STAG system, which combines a graphical drawing interface with a language which essentially allows a dialogue designer to define a 'rule' for each node in a transition network. Each rule is actually quite complex: it specifies the node it represents, the question to be asked, the various possible answers, and what action to carry out for each possible answer. Bateman expresses the view that users should construct their own dialogues. Whilst this may be a little radical for most tastes, there is undoubtedly room for users to have far more say in the shape dialogues take. One way to achieve this is to involve the user more fully in the design of the dialogue. The transition network clearly has a role to play here as a medium of interchange between the system builder and the user, because its simple concept and graphical representation make it easy for the non-technical user to grasp.

Once a large network has been installed, users could be allowed to customise their 'own' versions of the dialogue system. Whilst this might pose problems for system maintainability, it would also render systems more acceptable to users: for example, questions to which a user invariably gave the same answer could be struck from that user's version of the system.

5.5 THE SPECIFICATION

Bundy (1) has suggested an overall process of 'Translation, Synthesis and Inference.' Fig 5.2 is taken from (1). The major problem of the specification is to make the leap from the task specification supplied by the user to instructions which can be passed to the package which the IFE fronts. The key to the model shown in fig 5.2 is a set of 'methods.' Each of these methods represents an operation which the package may perform. These form the missing link between the desired effects as expressed in the task specification which the user has supplied, and the instructions which the IFE passes to the package. The situation is complicated by preconditions associated with methods. A method may only be applicable when other methods have been invoked (for example, the output of one method may be an essential input for another). Hence each precondition effectively adds a further desired effect to the task specification, thus spawning the invocation of further methods.

To sum up, desired effects are abstracted from the user's goals,   methods are initially selected by matching against those effects, but further methods may then be invoked to

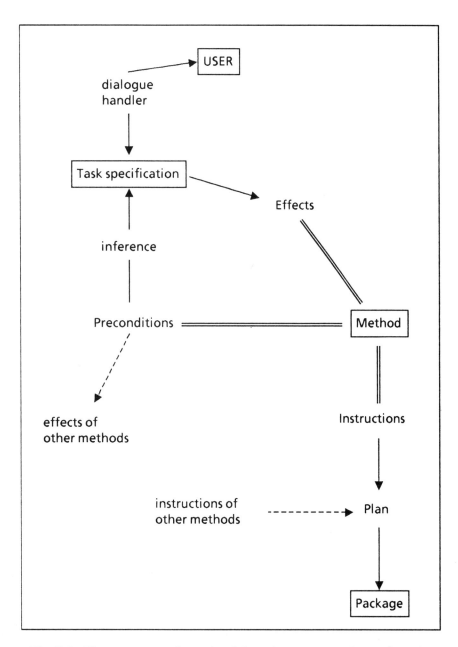

Fig 5.2 The process of synthesising the package input (Bundy
(1))

satisfy preconditions for the use of the top level methods.

When instructions have been generated to satisfy all the methods required, these instructions can then be combined to form an overall plan.

This simple model has limitations. The first level of complication occurs when the user's task specification or goals do not match exactly against any set of methods. In this case either it may be possible to effect a translation, or alternatively, clarifying dialogue with the user may ensue.

Clarifying dialogue is a technique which enables system and user to function more effectively by operating as a partnership. In general, such co-operative systems can gain wider understandings of user goals than are possible through just accepting the user's requests at their face value. Such systems attempt to address not just the explicit requests of users, but also their implicit assumptions. As an example, consider a system designed to carry out mathematical operations. A simplistic system, if asked the question;

> 'Is the product of matrix A with matrix B equal to 42 ?'

might reply

> 'No.'

A co-operative system could provide a more informative response, such as:

> 'The product of two matrices is a further matrix, not a number.'

Thus the system fills an educational role. In the case of co-operative IFEs, the education is likely to be in the form of knowledge about the target package, for example indicating the difference between failing to find the relevant information within a database and being unable to access the required information using the given database access routines. For the interested reader, a good example of a co-operative system is described by Kaplan (4).

Other systems enlist the user's aid in carrying out some of the operations. In particular, one may assist users in reformulating their task specifications to match the available methods. The 'Forms Helper' mentioned earlier is an example of such a system.

5.6 RUNNING THE PACKAGE

Provided that the previous stages have been concluded successfully, this should be relatively straightforward. One area of interest concerns the situation where a complex request necessitates the IFE instructing the package to perform several operations. In this case, a number of different groups of operations, possibly ordered differently, may each be sufficient to answer the query. The choice that must therefore be made is likely to be carried out on the basis of, for example, considerations of computational efficiency. In order to effectively make such choices it is helpful for the IFE to maintain a model of the package.

5.7 REPORTING BACK

Reporting back to users may require translation of the results obtained to make them compatible with the form in which the user's requests were originally phrased. This problem will be significant whenever a true natural language system is in use, and may be significant for other interfaces which allow the user to largely drive the interaction.

One situation where a translation may be necessary is that where the IFE has succeeded in meeting the user's requirements, but only by passing a complex set of instructions to the package.An obvious point here is that the user is unlikely to be interested in the intermediate steps and results. However, reporting only information pertaining specifically to the user's goals runs risks. If a user has provided ambiguous instructions through a natural language interface, and the system has misinterpreted those instructions, the error might not be noticed. By way of contrast, if the IFE reports back the details of the approach used for meeting the user's perceived demands, the mismatch is likely to be spotted. Furthermore, the user will have a better understanding of how the results were generated, and thus a better appreciation of other issues such as the range of situations over which those results are valid.

5.8 APPLICATION TYPES

The previous sections have provided a basic framework for discussion of IFEs. This section will look at some classes of application which can benefit from an IFE.

Several different types of application have been investigated. However, we will restrict ourselves to three main classes here.

The three areas to be discussed are:

- IFEs for large-scale conventional databases

- IFEs for complex statistical packages

- IFEs to enable the construction of computer models

5.8.1 IFEs for databases

The most important benefit which an IFE can confer upon a database system is 'data independence.' In other words, allowing the user to make queries of a database without the need to understand the database's internal organisation.

In considering the dialogue, one can make some observations peculiar to database IFEs. Firstly, whilst a number of database systems have incorporated natural language dialogue, the use of this approach in this particular area does pose unique problems. These are:

(i) Database users may well have not only a poor understanding of the database structure, but in the case of users who are not computer literate, a false one (arrived at, for example, by analogy with a paper-based filing system). A natural language system, which does not make obvious the constraints governing the types of queries which are answerable, does nothing to alleviate this problem.

(ii) Database users may often be regular users who are not trained typists. This may lead to a tendency to wish to shorten input, and thus to be useful a natural language system should handle ungrammatical input. In this context, ellipsis (see previous chapter) should always be handled. Similarly, typing errors should be quickly detected, and easily correctable.

(iii) A straightforward natural language system places a substantial cognitive load on a user, who must remember the correct names for items such as record field names.

The last two of these can often be alleviated by handling ellipsis, using spelling correction, or using some semantic knowledge describing the domain. At a more prosaic level, a good selection of synonyms is highly useful (particularly when a number of the users are occasional rather than regular).

Another problem arises when the user's implicit assumptions are erroneous. This can actually occur in IFEs of all types, but is most common amongst database systems. The problem can be addressed by the use of co-operative systems. In the specific case of IFEs for databases, however, further efforts can be made. The basis for this is the use of 'semantic affinities.'

The term 'semantic affinities' is used to describe concepts which are semantically close in some sense (for an example, see later). By specifiying these affinities as transformations, one can provide an IFE capable of transforming a query which cannot be answered directly into one capable of being answered. The new query may well not provide one hundred per cent accurate information, but may prove adequate.For further information on just one theoretical approach to the transformation problem, see (5).

As an example of the use of semantic affinities, consider the query 'Which sales staff live in Hampshire ?' A database not containing the home addresses of sales staff would not be able to answer the query directly, but an IFE of the type suggested would start by transforming the query to 'which sales staff work for the Hampshire regional office ?' Importantly, this query must be echoed to the user, allowing the users to make their own assessment of the validity of the answer the system finally produces. In this case, the system would falsely supply sales staff who live outside Hampshire and commute in, and miss those who live inside and commute out. For all that, the answer to the query would be largely correct, and provided users were clearly informed of the limitations of the response, they could often make good use of it.

Clearly emerging is the importance of matching what the system has done to what the user thinks it has done – reducing the cognitive dissonance. This problem is acute in complex systems of all kinds, and must therefore be expected where an IFE is in use – the presence of an IFE predicates the existence of two complex systems, the IFE itself and the complex package it is providing an interface to.

All of the foregoing discussion of IFEs for databases has been concerned with systems which enable the user to interrogate the contents of the database. Ideally, the user should also be able to ask questions about the database; its structure, the kinds of information stored in it, and so on. This involves the IFE maintaining yet another model – this one describing the domain about which the database holds information.

This information can be used without the user's knowledge to make more efficient queries. For example, the query;

'Which staff members have beards ?'

coupled with the domain knowledge

'Only men have beards'

could lead to the more efficient query

'Which male staff members have beards ?'

Finally, it is worth considering the potential for making queries which simply were not possible before. This is going rather beyond the concept of an IFE as described before, but the ability of expert system techniques to handle vague concepts can enable a system to respond to queries such as;

'Please list all the sales staff living in the South, and performing well last year'

with an ordered list of personnel; sorted according to how well they fit this vague definition. Using a precise, conventional interface, one might ask

'Please list all the sales staff living south of Watford, and earning more than £5000 last year'

This would run the danger that a salesman living 1 mile south of Watford, who made £51000, would be selected, whereas a saleswoman living 1 mile north of Watford, earning £100000, would be overlooked. The vague system would identify both, and additionally rank them suitably.

5.8.2 IFEs for complex statistical packages

There are a large number of complex statistics packages available today. The interfaces to these packages vary from the good to the bad, but virtually all make the assumption that the user knows which particular analysis techniques are relevant to the experiment or data which is being analysed. This may often not be the case. Apart from identifying which techniques are appropriate to given data, an IFE to a statistical package may address other issues.

Firstly, it is useful, having identified a number of different techniques which would all work, to carry on to select the best. This is analogous to the problem described earlier, of selecting the most efficient means of carrying out a database enquiry.

Secondly, the user may well wish to investigate the methods available in terms of the assumptions which they make. Most statistical methods make assumptions about issues such as the extent to which the individual data items are independent, and so on. Interestingly, knowledge about the domain (statistical analysis) which is not directly relevant to the use of the package being front-ended has often been found to be of much value to the user in this case. This is essentially because the inability to use a complex package may stem from lack of understanding of the subject as well as of the package.

Thirdly, intelligence may be required in presenting the results. The kind of user who requires an IFE may not understand the reliability of a correlation which has been shown to be significant to ' a certainty of 97.5 %.' This problem is exacerbated by the fact that, for example, such a statement would be regarded as good proof by a social scientist, but not by a physicist. A good dynamic user model can be used here, and the system will, by this stage, have sufficient information to gauge the depth of the user's statistical knowledge

5.8.3 IFEs for modelling problems

In essence, the problem that IFEs can address here is how to allow people who are neither mathematicians nor programmers to construct usable mathematical models.

In addition to the normal elements of an IFE which we have covered earlier, new elements such as consistency checkers will be required. These can operate at two levels. Firstly, logical/mathematical consistency, checking such things as factors that do not influence anything. Secondly, an IFE may have knowledge about a specific domain (for example, see ECO (2), described later in this chapter). Such knowledge may have other uses, including helping the user during the model construction process, not asking questions with 'obvious' answers, and so on.

Weiss et al (8) have identified some guiding principles for the development of such systems;

' Be careful when offering advice. One must not offend a truly expert user, yet help should be available to those requiring it.

Modularity is very important. The final system will be ever changing as new modelling results and methods become known.

It must be relatively easy to add the neccesary back end components, as well as updating the knowledge base.

The original back end software may require some reorganisation in order to fit the new framework.'

Perhaps the most important point emerging from the foregoing is the importance of treating as part of the knowledge base that knowledge which describes the modelling methods, and hence governs the back end of the IFE.

Before leaving this topic, it is interesting to reflect that building a model of some kind is somewhat akin to the process of constructing a knowledge base. Both must be internally self-consistent, both contain information only available to experts in a field, and both are sufficiently complex for it to be possible for far-reaching errors not to be immediately apparent. Most of what has been said in this context is applicable to the building of interfaces to the knowledge in expert systems; these interfaces will be used long after the departure of the knowledge engineer. An example of such an interface is described in the case study on ESCORT in Chapter 8, where the knowledge can easily be thought of as a model of how a process plant works.

5.9 PRACTICAL EXAMPLES

This section provides examples of practical work which has been carried out in the areas described above. The systems described have not neccesarily been selected as the best known, or as the most advanced examples of their kind, but to demonstrate the range of approaches which is available.

5.9.1 Karma – an IFE for a database

The Karma system was built by P. Bose and M. Rajinikith (6). Karma provides an IFE to a relational database. For the reader not familiar with the relational concept, a relational database contains data organised in tables, known as relations. Each column in one of these tables or relations is an attribute. Thus each row (known as a tuple) consists of a set of attribute values. An example usage might be:

Relation: car

Attributes: cost, top speed, manufacturer

Tuple: Ford Escort, Austin Mini

To use such a database, the user must understand this concept, must know relation and attribute names, and probably the syntax of a formal query language.

The underlying design goals of the system builders were to make such a database accessible to inexperienced users, and to help users to refine their initially vague requirements. The *sine qua non* of Karma is the use of a 'retrieval by reformulation' strategy. This strategy was introduced earlier (section 5.3).

Bose and Rajinikith make a distinction between two stages of the reformulation process. Firstly, an interactive process between user and system to convert the user's possibly incomplete conceptual requirement into a complete screen-based query. Secondly, a system reformulation to generate an efficient and executable query.

Karma is implemented using a WIMP interface (see Chapter 2). Various displays ease the cognitive load on the user, including graphical representations of the result of the last query, and a reminder of the last query actually used.

Karma's model of the domain is defined using a frame-based hierarchy. A sample of this representation is shown in fig 3.2.

Bose and Rajinikith make the interesting claim that this representation allows Karma to overcome certain inherent deficiencies in the relational database concept. They present the following argument. In order to distinguish between two subclasses of a more general class, the pure relational model must define these as separate relations, or must define a general relation where some attributes are simply not applicable. For example, consider the definition of a database of writing implements. One either defines pencils and biros as entirely separate relations, ignoring the fact that both are writing implements, or one defines a single writing implement relation, where some attributes will only apply to either pencils or Biros. In the first case, one fails to reflect adequately the similarity of function between the two. In the second case, the need to describe the refill of a Biro means that attributes are provided for all pencils which will never possess a value for any pencil. Neither approach describes the semantics of the situation accurately. By way of contrast, the 'is a' relationship in the frame-based hierarchy (see fig 3.2) describes the situation both clearly and economically, by allowing inheritance of general attributes from more general classes (eg. car) to more specific (eg. Austin).

The object hierarchy provides a model of the domain which the user may arguably find easier to comprehend than the database itself. The formulation of a query in such a domain becomes little more than the specification of a highly specific class, and reformulation can proceed by adding and removing super-classes to that class. Thus Karma can easily support the user in the formulation and reformulation of queries about the domain. This section of Karma's performance corresponds to the dialogue and task specification described earlier in the generalised model of IFE architecture.

The remaining task for Karma is the generation of an efficient query. The knowledge required to perform this translation is represented as a number of constraints of the type described earlier as semantic constraints. There are additionally a number of generally applicable rules which relate to general tasks within the process of generating an efficient query. An example of such a heuristic as described in (7) is a 'subsumption-heuristic.' This can be paraphrased as saying that one may obtain all members of a class by taking the union of the members of all its subclasses. An example of a possible use of this heuristic is shown in fig 5.3.

In summary, then, Karma is a system which provides intelligent assistance to a database user. The important concepts are:

- a model of the domain, independent of the database. This model offers some improvement in conceptual clarity over the database alone

- a clear distinction between helping the user to formulate queries (dialogue) and generating queries for the database (converting a task specification into package instructions)

- a dialogue which is clearly interactive. Results of previous queries form the basis for the next, more accurate query, as the process of reformulation proceeds.

5.9.2 REX – an IFE for a statistical package

REX (Regression EXpert) has been developed by AT & T Bell Laboratories. AT & T produce a statistical package called 'S,' which carries out, amongst other routines, regression analysis. Regression is a technique for fitting a straight line to a group of points, but which makes a number of assumptions; for example, that the group of points are somewhat compact.

An experienced regression expert can check these assumptions and can also correct the situation when one or

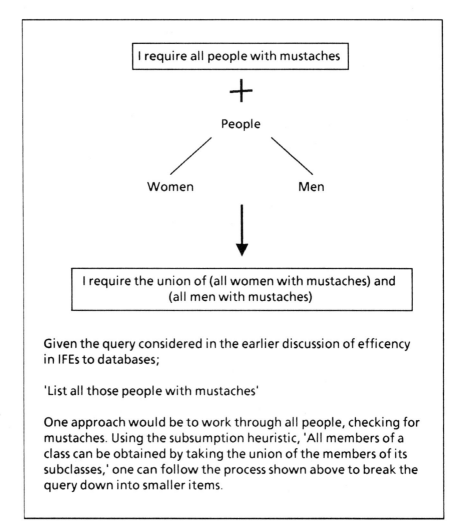

Fig 5.3 Using the subsumption heuristic

more of the assumptions are violated. REX contains knowledge which it can apply to correct for inadvertent assumption violation on the part of novice users.

REX is useful to AT & T, because it dramatically increases (AT & T claim a factor of two) the number of people who can use the package 'S.' Besides checking the validity of assumptions, REX can analyse the output of 'S' with a view to providing any neccesary fixes.

REX also attempts to inform. As it proceeds, it can explain the significance of its instructions to 'S' and what these are contributing towards realising the user's goals. This is somewhat limited; the explanations are produced in typical rule format, by producing a chain of reasoning drawn directly from the rules fired (with all the limitations that implies - see Chapter 6).

AT & T typifies REX's users as people 'who had one course in statistics 10 years ago.' It enables scientific researchers to concentrate on their own disciplines, freeing them from the need to become partial experts in the field of statistics.

5.9.3 ECO - an IFE for constructing ecological models

This system is intended to allow ecologists to build mathematical models of ecological systems without the need for them to possess either mathematical or programming skills. Such models are of significant practical importance in aiding with management decisions.

The system is described by its builders in (2). The goals they set themselves were described by Uschold in another paper (15). At that early stage, two items were seen as essential features:

- An intermediate representation of the model, which should be easily accessible to the user for inspection and modification, as well as being precise enough to form an input to a program generator so that the model can be run.

- A large knowledge base of ecological data and relationships. This is of central importance, as both system and user will require access to this item.

The system is restricted to 'Systems Dynamics' models. Systems Dynamics models use a highly defined schematic representation, which is intended for ecologists to use without mathematical formulae. This makes it an ideal choice for an intermediate representation - the user can understand it, and one can build on it to provide the precision required by a program generator.

In the System Dynamics world, there are a number of

compartments, with pipes running between them. Each pipe has a valve which governs flow. There is one special compartment in any System Dynamics world, the source/sink, which represents the outside world.

The valves on pipes mentioned earlier are controlled by 'flow expressions'. These may be arbitrarily complex, and are usually modules with inputs and outputs. The inputs may be external values such as rainfall, temperature, etc., or may in turn be the outputs of further modules. These dependencies define 'how the model works'.

5.9.3.1 ECO's structure

The overall structure of ECO is shown in fig 5.4. One of the system's strengths is the clear separation of the intermediate representation. This consists of a pair of directed graphs, which represent the flow within a System Dynamics module, and the dependencies between the modules underlying the flow expressions. An example, drawn from (2), is shown in fig 5.5.

The main system consists of 4 compartments and 4 flows, and models the process of sheep grazing in an area. Arrows not connected at one end or another are understood to be connected to the sink/source. A second graph, which is acyclic, then defines the dependencies between the modules: each node is a module. More detail concerning the intermediate representation is shown in fig 5.5.

The ecological knowledge base is used to support the dialogue between user and system which enables the construction of a System Dynamics module. It allows some activities to be performed automatically, such as checking that modules are being used in an appropriate ecological context, or that the units are compatible.

There are three elements of the knowledge base:

(i) Module Library: this describes each of the modules available for users to incorporate with their models

(ii) Entities: all the objects which the system can contain (grass, sheep, etc.)

(iii) Process Library: grazing, respiration, etc. This section has

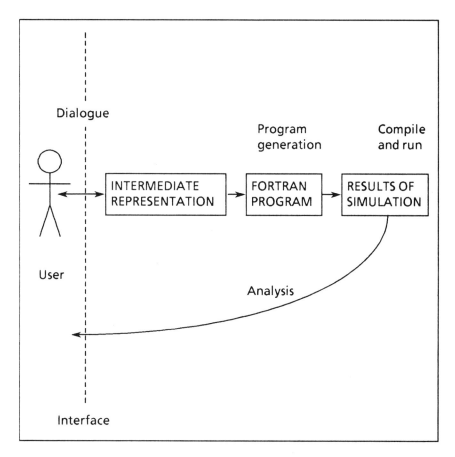

Fig 5.4 Structure of ECO

rules which describe which entities may take part in a given process.

A browser to the ecological knowledge base was constructed (see Robertson et al., (6)). This relies on a frame based hierarchy (that is, where each link in the hierarchy can be read as 'is-a'). Thus as the users move down this hierarchy, they encounter items of increasing specificity. Selecting an entity causes all items of knowledge which refer to it to be displayed for inspection. Further selection of entities then reduces the set of available records, or conversely deselection increases it.

Such an approach to knowledge 'browsing' is of interest in

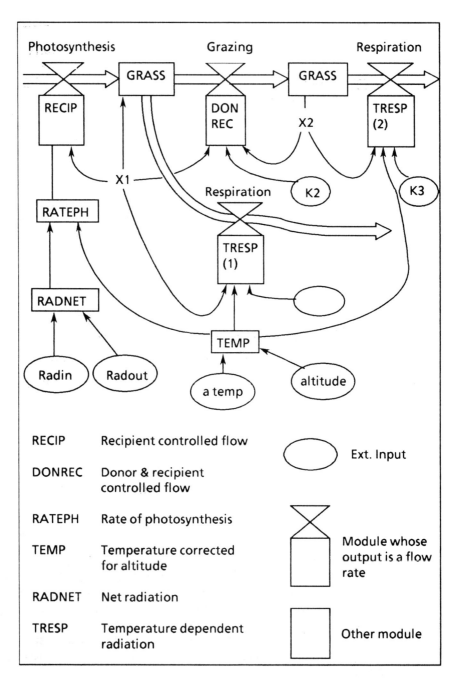

Fig 5.5 Example of a System Dynamics module (Uschold (2))

any domain where knowledge is loosely structured. Given a graphical display and an object-oriented development environment, one can very swiftly construct the appropriate mechanisms.

The third item of interest is the dialogue system proper. This allows the construction of the intermediate representation of the model by means of a dialogue between user and system. Essentially the user makes statements about the model he or she wishes to build.

One of the main strengths of ECO is the naturalness of its intermediate representation. This makes the potential value of allowing the user to interact directly with a graphical representation all the more significant. Unfortunately, Prolog, the language used for the development of ECO, is not well suited to the construction of such systems.

Nevertheless, ECO does have a straightforward dialogue. Six kinds of statement only may be made by the user:

DOES: <entity> <process> <entity>
                   eg. sheep graze grass

USES: specifies how a quantity is to be computed, ie
                   select a module, add the inputs and outputs,
                   etc.

SET: like USES, but specific to leaf nodes (ie SET
                   an input to a node to be a fixed value)

SPLIT/UNIFY: Either specify that two inputs are the same,
                   or that one input, previously held to be global,
                   actually represents two different values

DISPLAY: Display the model.

By allowing only a small range of statements, the following benefits accrue:

● typing is minimised

- parsing user input is fairly trivial

- no confusion arises over the user's intentions

Also, as mentioned before, the knowledge base is used for checking by the dialogue management system. For example, the system knows that grazing involves animals and plants, and it knows which way the energy flows. This checking process is extended to fill in obvious gaps. Less obvious gaps (for example, graph nodes which are eventually left unused) can also be flagged to the user.

Thus, the user has the facilities to build, change and extend the intermediate representation of a model. Program generation (the 'back end' of the system) is relatively straightforward: each module is a Fortran statement, and the acyclic nature of the graph linking modules enables one to order the calling of these subroutines such that those whose inputs are outputs of others are not called until later. The links in the graph indicate how assignments should be matched.

The contents of the compartments can be updated by adding incoming flows and subtracting outgoing ones.

5.9.3.2 Conclusions

Uschold et al. correctly identify the choice of the intermediate representation as crucial, noting a wide terminological gap between ecologist and model. The use of a graph is often worthwhile when attempting to represent a complex structure   in a way which users find natural. The advantages include:

(i) the ability to hide detail
(ii) the ability to spot inconsistencies and errors in structure
(iii) ease of modification

Secondly, the concept of a domain specific knowledge base available to both sdystem and user is of general applicability.

5.10 FURTHER READING

It is important to recognise that research into IFEs is still at an early stage. Furthermore, the different IFEs are very disparate: the sum total of the area is a lot of good ideas , rather than a few universal guiding principles. Generalised structures such as the one discussed at the beginning of this chapter are only just beginning to emerge. Anyone attempting to build an IFE would be well advised to look at previous efforts in a related field. What follows, then, is a short list of interesting papers.

1. Tai, F N et al., (1982) 'RABBIT: An Intelligent Database Assistant', AAAI-82

   - A seminal paper which presented one of the earliest clear descriptions of the browsing by reformulation approach described briefly in this chapter.

2. Bennet J S & Englemore R, (1979) 'SACON: A knowledge-based consultant for structural analysis', IJCAI-79

   - An example of a system which dynamically constructs a transition network using production rules.

3. Hopgood F R A & Duce D A, (1980) 'A production rule system approach to interactive program design' in 'Methodology of Interaction', North-Holland

   - A further example of a dialogue based on production rules.

4. Bateman, R F, (1983) 'A translator to encourage user modifiable man-machine dialogue' in 'Designing for Human-Computer Communications', Academic Press

5. Alty, J L, (1984) 'Path Algebras - a useful CAI/CAL analysis technique', Proc of Computer-assisted learning symposium, P R Smith (ed.), Pergamon Press

- Two examples which use transition networks for dialogue handling

5.11 CONCLUSIONS

Intelligent front ends represent work at the leading edge of interface design. They amply illustrate the need to consider user requirements, user models, user limitations, and so on. We have tried to describe IFEs in such a way as to make it clear that they represent an area in which new technology is being used essentially to enable better use of older technology. Thus the technology can be seen both as evolutionary (as older systems are enhanced) and revolutionary (as the novel techniques of IKBS are introduced into many areas for the first time).

One of the ways in which this can happen occurs when the IFE helps to educate or train the users of a system. This is facilitated by the provision of explanations of an IKBS's activities which are fed back to the user. The role of such explanations is explored further in the next chapter.

5.12 REFERENCES

1. Bundy A, (1984) 'Intelligent Front Ends', BCS '84

2. Uschold et al., (1984) 'An IFE for ecological modelling', ECAI '84

3. Feigenbaum & Barr, (1982) 'The handbook of Artificial Intelligence Vol II', HeurisTECH Press

4. Kaplan S J, (1979) 'Co-operative responses from a portable natural language query system', Univ of Pennsylvania

5. Zarri G P, (1985) 'Adding an expert system component to the natural language interface of relational databases', Proc. 1st International Expert System Conf.

6. Robertson D et al, (1985) "The ECO Browser," BCS '85

7. Bose P & Rajinikith M, (1986) 'Karma - An intelligent assistant to a database system', Expert System Journal, Jan 1986

8. Weiss S et al, (1982) 'Building Expert Systems for controlling computer programs', AAAI-82

10. Ramsay A, 'Dialogue handling in an Intelligent Front End', report to 2nd workshop of IFE theme of Alvey IKBS stream, 1984

11. Alty J, "The application of path algebras to encourage user-modifiable man-machine dialogue, Research report no. 131, (University of Strathclyde, Dept of Computer Science)

12. Alty J, (1984) 'Use of path algebras in an interactive adaptive dialogue system', 2nd Alvey workshop on IFEs

13. Bateman R F, (1983) "A translator to encourage user-modifiable man-machine dialogue", in Sime M E, "Designing for human computer communications" (Academic Press London)

14. "The Alvey Programme Annual Report," 1986, IEE

15. Uschold, M., "An Expert System for ecological modelling," the Alvey IFE Workshop No 1, (1983)

6

Explanation and help in expert systems

6.1 INTRODUCTION

This chapter addresses a particular aspect of the user interface, common to most expert systems: the ability of such systems to justify their expert advice. This chapter will also consider the many other types of dialogue which an expert system can use in attempting to satisfy some basic goal. There are few practical examples of such systems. This is an indication of the very early stage of development of this aspect of expert systems. Indeed, it would be fair to say that the majority of expert systems provide inadequate support in this area, which is ironic when so many attempts to justify the value of expert systems revolve around their ability to provide explanations.

6.2 THREE LEVELS OF EXPLANATION AND DIALOGUE

Explanation and other related user-system dialogues can occur at 3 levels. At the lowest level, one may ask very specific questions, asking the system to justify a particular piece of advice. In this case, one is asking the system for the items within its knowlege base which connect the system's proferred advice with the domain in its current state, and the user's goals. A system may be required to support many different question types at this level. Mc Donald (1) has identified six query types supported by one system:

- Why or how a conclusion has been reached

- How to further substantiate a conclusion

- What must be done to prove a hypothesis

- What information provided is contradictory

- What information has been provided so far

- What background information pertains to the current situation

One can conceive of others that might be required, two of particular interest being:

- Why was a particular conclusion NOT reached

- Is X the right conclusion

Which question types are important will be influenced by both the application and the user's knowledge and skills.

The common factor which groups these explanations at the lowest level (1) is that they are all questions which make no reference to the high level reasoning strategy employed by the expert system. This low level view of the reasoning can best be understood by considering an expert system which is built using simple rules. In this case, appeal to rules of logic would enable the system to answer most such questions without reference to the system's problem solving strategy. All that would be required would be the chain of rules linking problem and solution.

Moving up to a higher level (level 2), the explanation system considers questions of strategy. Many expert systems have either a trivial strategy or an implicit strategy not freely available for inspection. For example, many rule-based systems determine the answer to the strategy problem 'which rule should be tried next' by applying the strategy rule 'whichever candidate rule is closest to the top of the knowledge base'. Ideally, the system builder should explicitly represent the strategic knowledge that led to the rules being placed in a particular order. Unfortunately, this rarely happens, and the control knowledge is represented implicitly by the ordering of the rules. Thus the much vaunted 'transparency' of expert systems only extends to the raw knowledge, and not to the control of its use. Such systems are clearly unable to provide such level 2 explanations.

However, many workers are now starting to construct systems which do answer these criticisms. In many cases the change has been motivated by a desire to use more complex approaches to solving problems, rather than with the direct aim of providing more supportive dialogue. We shall investigate some of the possibilities which this explicit representation provides later in this chapter.

Finally, at a third level, a system may be asked to explain the soundness of an item within its knowledge base. In other words, rather than justifying the application of knowledge in a particular way, the system is called upon to explain the justification for the inclusion of a particular piece of knowledge in the knowledge base at all. Clancy (2) considers such a system for a physician. He concluded that such justifications are not part of a physician's everyday reasoning process. In other words, the physician often doesn't need to know why his knowledge works, and may even have forgotten. It is enough that it does work, and generates the right answers.

In the physician's case, then, such a 'level 3' explanation is not required in everyday practice. Clancy, however, was concerned with teaching physicians, and a student needs such a level of explanation. We shall later consider the general applicability of this type of explanation. We will also consider the relationship between this type of explanation, and the lowest level mentioned earlier.

The three levels or types of explanation we have identified are summarised in fig 6.1.

Level	Explanation
1	Presenting the chain of reasoning constructed by the system
2	Explanation of the reasons why a particular chain of reasoning was constructed rather than another
3	Justification for individual steps within the chain of reasoning used by the system

Fig 6.1 Levels of explanation

6.3 LEVEL 1 - ASKING WHY

We will now investigate level 1 explanations in more detail. Consider the extract from a rule-based knowledge base shown in fig 6.2.

Consider what happens when this knowledge base is combined with a simple backward-chaining inference engine. The resulting expert system is given the query 'what is a suitable drink ?'. The system first attempts to choose a rule which might answer the query. The most likely choice is rule 1 (as we have said earlier, most shells like to work from the top of the knowledge base). This will lead the system to set itself a second goal, namely 'try to prove that nature is depressed'. This will cause rule 2 to fire, and two new goals will be acquired: 'try to prove TV choice is current affairs' and 'try to prove financial status is poor'. The next step will be to ask the user to tell the system what his favourite TV program is. At this stage the user may be able to ask 'Why (am I being asked that question) ?'. The kind of response typical of many current systems might be:

'I am asking about TV programs in order to satisfy rule 2.

Rule 2 says:

If favourite TV program is current affairs

Rule 1   If nature is depressed
         then drink is gin

Rule 2   If favourite TV program is Current Affairs
         and financial status is poor
         then nature is depressed

Rule 3   If nature is happy
         then drink is champagne

Rule 4   If time of year is Christmas
         then drink is port

Question 1   What is your favourite TV program ?

Question 2   Is it Christmas time ?

Fig 6.2 Rule-based knowledge

and financial status is poor
then nature is depressed

I need to know about nature in order to satisfy rule
1.

Rule 1 says:

If nature is depressed
then drink is gin

I need to know about drink because you asked about
drink.'

This sequence demonstrates a number of deficiencies of
current expert system dialogues, and the abilities of these
systems to explain their actions. For example, the user can see

that admitting to a liking for current affairs will lead the system to an attempt to establish the user's financial status. The user may know that this will involve a lengthy question and answer session, and further be certain that the outcome will be that rule 2 is inapplicable. The user will either be forced into a frustating interchange, or may even be tempted to lie about his favourite TV program in an attempt to short-circuit the reasoning process. The first is annoying: the second may cause erroneous results, perhaps due to interactions the user has not foreseen. What is required, of course, is a more flexible, mixed initiative dialogue (see Chapter 3), which enables the user to redirect the system's line of reasoning.

Secondly, the user may be dimly aware of the existence of a rule such as rule 4, and ask the question 'why isn't port being considered ?', or 'why am I not being asked about the time of year ?'. Equally, should the user turn out to be depressed, the system is likely to recommend a glass of gin. The question 'why not port ?' is still valid.

The wish to ask why not is typical of many expert system users. For example, consider MASES (3). The system is designed to advise on the selection of microcomputer database packages. In many cases, the question the human expert would be asked, after making a recommendation, would be along the lines of:

> '... and Jane down the corridor has got dBase III, and she reckons it's marvellous. Why can't I use that instead ?'

However, the system's ability to answer the question 'why not ?' is often severely restricted. In the MASES case, the need was felt so sorely that the entire knowledge base was expressed in an unnatural way in order to render it possible to answer this query using a rule-based shell.

In general, the straightforward trace of rules cannot begin to answer this question. The best effort we could expect from our drinks adviser might be:

> 'Not port, because although there are rules that apply to port, the programmer chose to put them closer to the bottom of the knowledge base, and the gin rules closer to the top.'

Similar problems exist for most of the other query types quoted above.

However, the expansion of most expert systems to cover such queries is suprisingly simple. In many cases the omissions are due to oversight rather than difficulty. At the earliest stages of knowledge acquisition, the designer must also start to observe the user. This is general good practice which has many other benefits (see Chapters 7 and 10). In order to provide a truly 'expert' expert system, one should aim not just to duplicate the expert's knowledge and problem-solving capabilities, but also to provide the ability to support the same range of dialogue as the human expert. This is a good example of the benefits which accrue from not constructing expert systems in isolation.

6.4 LEVEL 2 – EXPLAINING STRATEGY

There are many definitions of strategy. We will define strategy as a plan or method for achieving some goal. As has been described earlier, most of the existing rule-based expert systems operate a simple strategy for rule selection, and furthermore one which makes any strategic knowledge implicit, and therefore not available to the user. The selection of rules is chosen as an example, because for rule-based systems it is certainly the key to the strategy: it will make the difference between a plan that leads quickly and accurately to the goal, and one that may lead down many blind alleys.

Clancy provides a good analysis of the deficiencies of such a system (2). He uses MYCIN as an example of a system which is hamstrung by its lack of an explicit strategy. MYCIN, whilst proving successful at identifying blood diseases, has not been useful for training. The main problem is that students need to learn problem-solving techiques, rather than discrete facts. These problems led to the development of NEOMYCIN, which implements an approach to the explicit representation of strategic knowledge. NEOMYCIN contains 'tasks' and 'metarules'. A task may represent either a top-level (ie user) goal, or some sub-goal of the system. A metarule is a straightforward if-then rule, used in a data-driven fashion. In other words, when its premise becomes true, it fires and carries out some action. This information is in addition to the domain-specific knowledge, also represented as rules, which is used to satisfy the goals and arrive at a suitable diagnosis.

The system functions as follows. A user goal is set up as a task. The existence of that task may invoke a metarule, which may in turn generate further sub-tasks. Ultimately a sub-task will be invoked which can be satisfied by the invocation of the base-level, MYCIN-like rule interpreter.

In her description of NEOMYCIN's explanation system, Warner-Hasling (4) distinguishes between the questions 'why' and 'how'. In the context of a particular question, NEOMYCIN will answer the question 'Why are you asking that question ?' in either abstract or concrete fashion. Essentially, the why question asks 'Why are we carrying out this particular task at all ?', where the goal of the task is to obtain some piece of information. As stated earlier, a task is invoked by a metarule, and one therefore can now answer the question 'Why this task ?' along these lines:

'Because metarule X says that it is a good idea to get this information whenever a certain state of affairs exists, and that state does currently exist, as ...'

This is clearly more useful to a student attempting to assimilate what it is that enables the expert to diagnose blood diseases.

Note that the explanation of 'why' at the meta level takes place without reference to 'how' (for example, 'how' was the correct diagnosis reached) in terms of the domain knowledge about diseases. Thus the system can explain the problem-solving strategy employed by the expert without reference to the specific case. This can help a student, who 'can't see the wood for the trees' when seeking to understand an expert's thought processes.

As has been implied, NEOMYCIN also allows the question 'HOW ?'. This will explain previously completed tasks. There is an interesting symmetry between these two features, which Warner-Hasling neatly highlights:

'A WHY explanation essentially states the premise of the metarule: this is exactly the reason the metarule succeeded. A HOW explanation is a statement of the action of the metarule: this is exactly what was done.'

Naturally, the user still has access to the standard WHY facility, which produces a trace of the rules fired by the low-level interpreter.

NEOMYCIN illustrates some of the advantages of explicit representation of strategy. Apart from the fact of the separation of strategy from the domain-specific knowledge in use, the strategy itself is remarkably abstract, leading to the suggestion that some approaches to strategy may be generally applicable across a range of domains. This topic will be pursued in more depth later in this chapter.

Finally, before leaving NEOMYCIN, it is worthwhile to consider the problems of explaining metarules (in other words, rules about when and how to apply other rules). For example, we suggested that users often like to ask questions like 'WHY NOT ?'. This is a difficult question to answer, essentially because the chain of reasoning curently favoured does not have any bearing on this question. The use of metarules largely alleviates this at one level. This is because one can explain the strategic decisions that led the system not to consider pursuing a particular avenue of investigation. Nevertheless, we are left with the same problems at the metalevel. For example, consider the drinks selection knowledge base of fig 6.2. Given the metarule 'ask about the factor which affects the most rules in the knowledge base pertaining to the current goal' (in this case selecting a drink), we can explain why the first question attempts to establish the user's nature. Equally, we can explain that a question about the time of year was not asked: 'because it only affects one of the drinks in the knowledge base'. However, when asked why this particular strategy was invoked, or why another was not,we are back to the same question. The cynic might ask why there aren't metametarules to explain the metarules. The simple answer is that one has to stop at some stage. However, this problem does explain some of the appeal of generalised heuristics for problem solving, because like the example suggested above, these are likely to appeal to common sense and thus users will be happier to accept them without questioning.

McDonald (1) describes a system intended to identify military munitions. The system is implemented as an inference network. Each node is either a hypothesis or question. Each link has a dual function, representing the logical and investigative relationship between the nodes. The logical relationships are those normally found in such a network, and allow the propagation of truth in a fairly standard manner. Thus, relationships exist between necessary or sufficient conditions and their consequences, and a three valued (true, don't know and false) logic is used to propagate truth across the network.

The investigative relationships are quite separate. These indicate how the potential of a node is calculated. The potential of a node is a number in the range [-1,1], and represents the likelihood that the current (don't know) state of of the node will eventually change to true or false. The potential has two uses. Firstly, it can be used to identify the goals most worthy of further investigation, and secondly the best way to investigate them.

For each link between nodes, two measures of support are recorded: these represent the effect which the change in potential of an antecedent node has upon the potential of a consequent. In this way, changes in potential ripple through the network.

These potentials then form the basis for strategy decisions. Strategy is based upon heuristics such as:

> 'the two top goals have nearly the same potential - select a question to distinguish between them'

In the context of the current discussion, this has two important implications. Firstly, the strategy-level heuristic can be used to explain why a particular question is being asked. For example:

> 'I'm asking about the number of fins because the bomb is likely to be either X or Y, and the number of fins will enable me to distinguish between the two'

Secondly, the potential measures enable the system to explain its choice of goals. Interestingly, it turns out, just as in the NEOMYCIN case, that the control knowledge takes the form of very general heuristics, which are not domain specific.

There is another aspect of the design of systems which embody metalevel reasoning which is of interest to the student of Human Factors. This is the way in which users are able to employ the system in more powerful ways as their knowledge grows. This is important, because it involves a mode of operation similar to that used in teacher/pupil relations. As knowledge grows, so the questions become more taxing, and we seek to understand deeper levels.

Metamodelling, providing rules about rules, is a very important feature of adaptive systems. We have previously described some of the issues involved in sophisticated user modelling, and these are analogous to some of the problems with metareasoning outlined here.

To conclude this discussion of strategy explanation, we should ask what are the lessons for the knowledge engineer. We have seen that explicit representations of strategic knowledge and problem solving techniques are crucial to providing some depth of cognitive support. This is particularly so in an environment where the user and the machine are co-operating to solve a problem. The ability of expert systems to provide co-operative problem solving distinguishes them from more conventional systems. In order for the users to operate effectively they must understand what the current goals are, and what is their relevance to the eventual goal. Finally, it appears that many strategy heuristics are domain independent. This is undoubtedly an advantage, because it lessens the need to provide explanations to human users who are more likely to accept such rules as 'common sense'.

6.5 LEVEL 3 - JUSTIFYING RULES

We now consider the problems involved with supplying justifications of the underlying rationale for a rule's existence. Clancy (2) identifies four types of rule found in the MYCIN system:

Identification rules - which classify objects by their properties. For example;

'If X has a moustache then X is male'

Causal rules - which link cause and effect. For example;

'If it rains then the grass will grow'

World fact rules - which are based on general knowledge of the world. For example,

> 'Spark plugs are not a likely cause of problems in fuel-injected engines'

Domain fact rules - which are statements of definitions which are true within the domain under consideration. For example,

> 'if the data arrived with the wrong check digits, then it must have got corrupted somewhere along the comms link'

In the context of explaining rules further, it is clear that only the causal rules require expansion. World facts should be part of any user's general knowledge (note the usefulness, once again, of appealing to 'common sense' and 'general knowledge'). Definitions and properties will only be required to be stated; it makes no sense to ask WHY a definition is as it is, or WHY some object has the properties it does.

The causal rule can usefully be regarded as a shortened form of a more complex explanation of some phenomenon. Consider the scenario shown in fig 6.3. The bucket is simultaneously filled from one pipe, and emptied by another. Now consider what happens when the valve is closed slightly. The level in the bucket will start to rise. At one level, one might say that:

> 'the level in the bucket is rising because the valve is partly closed'

As an explanation of this causal rule, the system could simply offer an expansion of the rule:

> 'the level in the bucket is rising because water is flowing in faster than it is flowing out. The outflow is higher than the inflow because the valve is partly closed'

Or in more detail:

> 'the level in the bucket is rising because water is flowing in faster than it is flowing out. The outflow is higher than the inflow because the outflow has been reduced below its normal level. The outflow has been reduced because there is an increased

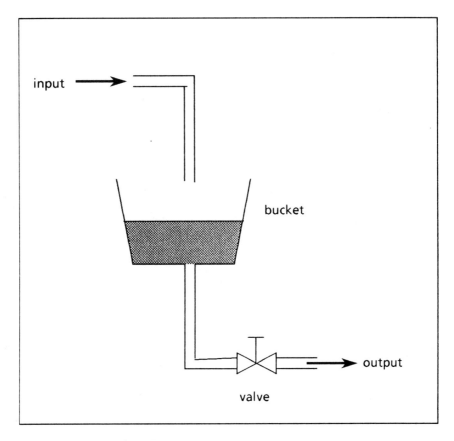

Fig 6.3 Scenario for causal explanations

obstruction in the outflow pipe. There is an increased obstruction because the valve is partly closed.'

This process of expansion can be continued ad nauseam, and is only bounded by the ability of modern physics to answer questions like 'why is there a gravitational force causing water to flow downward'. Clearly this level of detail is not necessary, either for providing an expert system with an adequate reasoning process, or for providing explanations to the majority of users. Equally, one must explain in enough detail to satisfy the user.

The question, then, is how to determine the appropriate level of detail for explaining a particular phenomenon to a particular user. Clancy (2) suggests that the best approach is to abstract a parallel with a familiar pattern of reasoning. This is justified by appealing to the idea that most causal rules relate to some process which has occurred. Therefore, it is possible to relate a particular rule's premise to some general idea of the path which the process being explained follows.

Previously we have focused largely on how to augment a difficult rule to make it more explainable. We have seen that a causal rule can be expanded to a number of smaller steps to allow a better explanation, or alternatively related to different but more general causal rules. Clearly the system builder cannot practically provide a breakdown of each rule to the finest possible grain size of detail provided for by the extent of human knowledge. Equally clearly, however, explanations at more than one level of detail can and should be provided. Assuming this approach were adopted, two questions now need to be answered. Firstly, how can we select an appropriate level of detail ? Secondly, how do we ensure that the various elements of an explanation constitute a uniform level of detail.

In answer to the first question, other techniques described earlier in this book can be employed, notably user modelling (see Chapter 3). Such approaches can be used when providing explanations to other people as well as the system's users. There is a need to consider the requirements of both the system developer/refiner (the knowledge engineer), and the expert who supplied the content of the knowledge base. This range requires that the level of each type of explanationwill vary for a given type of user: for example, the system developer will not be interested in any knowledge at a lower level than that at which the system reasons, but may make heavy use of facilities such as why not.

In the absence of a user model, one must take recourse to other approaches. Reasonable results can be obtained by making each substage of the explanation amenable to expansion. Even in this case, one can construct a rudimentary user model, which may be able to adapt itself to 'guess' at the level of expansion a user is likely to ideally wish for on the basis of past experience.

The converse of this problem - rules making too big a causal leap for users to follow - is that unacceptably small leaps may be made. In this case, the user will have no problems in understanding the explanation, but the high level of detail provided will cause frustration leading to an unwillingness to use the facility.

An example of a class of expert system for which this may be the case is those which employ 'naive physics'. Such systems are characterised by the combination of several very simple, common sense relationships, to form a large proof tree. Such systems succeed by applying very simple knowledge on a massive scale. The net results can be surprisingly complex: the sum effect of 100 small, common sense, inferences can be a surprising, difficult to follow conclusion. The naive approach to explanation, listing the 100 inferences, is unlikely to be welcomed by the user.

Eriksson & Johansson (5) make some interesting general comments about the 'transforming' of proof trees. They define definitional rules (analogous to Clancy's Domain fact rules described earlier), and suggest that proof trees can be made smaller and no less meaningful by the removal of the consequence of such rules. As an example, consider:

A is an ancestor of B if A is a parent of B   (1)

A is a parent of B if A is the father of B   (2)

Note that these are definitional rules. Hence, using Eriksson & Johansson's approach, we can take the original explanation

'Peter is an ancestor of John because Peter is a parent of John and
Peter is a parent of John because Peter is the father of John'

and replace it with

'Peter is an ancestor of John because Peter is the father of John'

This approach is attractive. The assumption it makes is, of course, that definitional rules are part of the general knowledge of the system's user.

Other approaches to foreshortening the proof are due to Clancy (2). He notes that where multiple premise clauses exist (ie. if A **and** B then C), some should be removed for the purposes of explanation. He identifies certain types of clause for which this is true.

The first of these are 'screening' clauses. These limit the applicability of a rule. For example:

> 'if X has claimed expenses
> and X has claimed hotel expenses
> then VAT may be reclaimed'

The second clause type is 'contextual' clauses. These 'describe the context in which the rule applies'. An example here might be:

> 'if transport is available
> and the weather is sunny
> then go to the beach

(one goes to the beach **because** it is sunny, **given** the context provided by the initial clause).

As well as deciding what to leave out of the full explanation, it is worth considering which elements of failed solutions to include. It may well be the case that the user stands to gain more understanding from the explanation of why one potential solution failed, than from the eventually successfull solution.

This is especially true of systems which employ some form of 'default reasoning' strategy: in other words, a system for advising on travel arrangements might reason 'I'll assume that the train will be the most economical means of transport until proved otherwise'. This strategy can prove useful. When it comes to explanations, however, this sytem, when asked 'why are you recommending rail travel' will reply 'because that is the default'. More useful would be a list of some of the items which might commonly cause the default to be over-ridden (for example, 'it is not the case that more than 3 people are travelling, and you are not travelling abroad, ...').

6.6 LAST THOUGHTS

The bulk of this chapter has focused on applying three levels of explanation to simple if-then rules. The question which may occur to many readers is to what extent this is applicable to expert systems which use other formalisms. In fact, most expert systems have either if-then rules or something similar. For example, semantic networks when analysed formally come down to much the same thing.

Problems may occur where parts of a knowledge base consist largely of procedures rather than declarative knowledge. This is because a procedure inevitably has elements of strategy implicit within itself.

Extensions to the ideas described above may be required for certain types of rule-based representation. For instance, none of the plethora of systems which make use of some numerical method or other for manipulating certainty factors, fuzzy set membership levels and the like, makes any attempt at explaining either what the numbers mean, how they are derived, or why the technique used to propagate the numbers across an if-then link is valid. This is probably because satisfactory answers to such questions don't exist - most builders of such systems prefer to point to the successful use of such techniques than to discuss their theoretical underpinnings. However, if such techniques are used to build a system, it must be accepted that the advantages gained by providing an explanation facility will be lost as the problems of explaining the numbers and their derivations are too difficult. This is one of the prime arguments against the use of such techniques in constructing expert systems - an expert system which provides high levels of problem-solving performance at the expense of the user's ability to understand it is likely to prove ultimately unsuccessful. Conversely, this is a powerful argument in favour of the alternative approach of providing an explicit representation of uncertainty. One such scheme is described in (6) by Fox.

At the very least, however, if a numerical technique is used for handling uncertainty, the system builder owes it to the users to make it clear whether the numbers are measuring the level of truth in a statement, or the level of accuracy of a statement, or something else again.

Lastly, other declarative knowledge formalisms should be considered. Object- and frame-based systems are relatively easy to explain at a logical level. Furthermore, most of the knowledge is analogous to either the definitional or Identification rule types described before - see fig 6.4. The

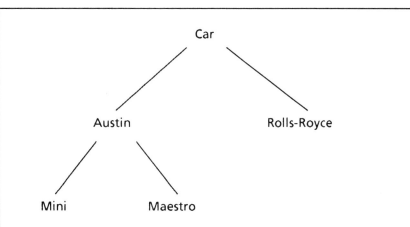

The link between Mini and Austin is normally read

    'A Mini is one type of Austin'

An alternative reading, in terms of a definitional rule, might be

    'If car X is a Mini then car X is an Austin'

The attributes (instance values or slots) of a frame are normally read as,
for example:

    'The price of a Rolls-Royce is high'

But could alternatively be read as identification rules such as:

    'If the price is high then it is likely that the car is a Rolls-Royce'

Fig 6.4 Definitional and identification knowledge in frame
hierarchies

comments for strategy and justification remain largely valid.

Rules generated by induction pose a particular problem for explanations. The difficulty is that the knowledge may not exist at all outside the computer system, and even if it does it may well not be in the same form as the version within the computer. The rules generated by the induction process are likely to be counter-intuitive, and similarly the chance that the system's behaviour does not fit in with the user's common-sense model of how to solve the problem is higher than normal. Precious little work seems to have been done in this area to date, and the subject requires further investigation. However, at least records should be kept of the events during the induction process – these may help to justify otherwise implicit strategy decisions, such as the ordering of the questions.

6.7 CONCLUSIONS

Explanations offer a useful extension to the user interface which can easily be provided in the context of an expert system. They provide knowledge about decisions and advice which may be useful for training, education, or to increase the faith users place in the conclusions reached.

We have raised some questions about how knowledge can be justified. Clearly this question relates to a process which takes place before an expert system can be built: knowledge acquisition. In the next chapter we focus on the knowledge acquisition process.

6.8 REFERENCES

1. McDonald R K, (1986) 'Factoring out investigative inferences', BCS 86

2. Clancy W J, (1983) 'The epistemology of a rule-based system: a framework for explanation,' Artificial Intelligence Vol 20

3. Cleal D M, (1984) 'Teaching computers by example,' CCTA News Jan 1984

4. Warner-Hasling D, (1983) 'Abstract explanations of strategy in a diagnostic consultation system,' Proc AAAI-83

5. Eriksson A & Johansson A-L, 'Neat explanations of proof trees,' Uppsala Univ

6. Fox J, (1985) 'Decision-making and Uncertainty in expert systems,' AI and Statistics workshop, Bell Labs.

7

Knowledge acquisition

7.1 INTRODUCTION

Knowledge acquisition or elicitation (we will use the two as synonyms, though some people refer to elicitation as simply gathering the information, whilst acquisition includes some interpretation) is one of the traditional bottlenecks in the design of expert systems and IKBSs. There are two central problems:

- how is knowledge obtained from the expert(s)

- how is that knowledge then structured to form an appropriate knowledge base.

Both problems are poorly understood and under-researched. A recent bibliographic summary contained some 10 entries under the heading of knowledge acquisition compared with over 70 entries (and one cross reference) for knowledge representation (1). Yet it is apparent that without acquisition there can be no representation.

Whilst comparatively little is known about knowledge acquisition it is generally seen as the key to the successful design of expert systems. A successful expert system must contain an embodiment of the expert's knowledge in a usable and correct form.

As expert systems are being built and successfully used, then knowledge acquisition is also being employed successfully. The problem is that there are so many different methods of eliciting knowledge that it is difficult to point to one prescriptive way of doing it. This chapter attempts to consider some of the methods in detail, outlining the pros and cons of each.

Knowlege acquisition is the process by which experts provide their expertise for expert systems. It is not necessary to use a knowledge engineer to elicit expertise. Some organisations believe that experts should act as their own knowledge engineers, whilst others believe that there are substancial benefits to be gained in providing an intermediary between the expert and the system.

We will distinguish four roles in the process of knowledge acquisition. These need not all be filled by different people, but for the purposes of this chapter four distinct roles will be considered.

Depending on which organisation is building the system these four roles may be more or less discrete. Some organisations believe that the expert should serve as both knowledge engineer and system builder as well as being the expert. However, the most important point, no matter in which way the roles are combined, is that the end-user must be involved. The expert/knowledge engineer/designer will, in general, be neither sufficiently knowledgeable nor inexperienced to represent the end-user. The only exception to this general rule is the case where one of the three (most commonly the expert) is to be the sole user of the system.

7.2 WHY KNOWLEDGE ACQUISITION IS DIFFICULT

We have already stated that knowledge acquisition is a problem. We will attempt to investigate why this is so.

the Expert	The expert possesses knowledge or expertise which is going to be uncovered and used to build an expert system.
the Knowledge Engineer	The knowledge engineer serves as an intermediary between the expert and the system designer. The knowledege engineer's task is to provide the designer with enough knowledge from the expert to allow the designer to produce at least an initial system, then to serve as an intermediary in the subsequent modification and enhancement of the system.
the System Designer	The system designer requires the expert's knowledge in a form which can be translated into an expert system. The designer might initially know nothing about the nature of the expertise yet will be required to produce a system which will satisfy the expert.
the User	The user is the person for whom the system has been built. Often the user has requirements which are markedly different from those of the other three and these requirements must be considered at an early stage. The construction of expert systems without user involvement might produce something which satisfies the expert but could only be used by the expert.

Experience should have taught us that knowledge is difficult to convey. We use many mechanisms to pass knowledge on. Speech, books, combinations of sight and sound are all used but rarely with anything approaching 100% success. If knowledge acquisition was easy, there would be less need for schools, universities and experts. Knowledge acquisition is a difficult task, even given experts who are expert at passing on knowledge, such as teachers.

Analogous to this is the difficulty in obtaining knowledge for the design of expert systems. The expert has knowledge, is often unaware of the nature of that expertise and knowledge and is required to convey that knowledge to a system designer who may have little or no experience with the underlying subject domain.

A knowledge engineer serves as a bridge between the domain expert and the system builder. The knowledge engineer's expertise is in eliciting knowledge from the expert and then translating it into terms which the system designer can understand.

Another problem with knowledge acquisition is the mismatch in levels between machines and humans. Machines require knowledge to be expressed explicitly at a lower, more detailed, level than humans. Human knowledge may not be expressed explicitly at this level but instead exist in a 'compiled' format where only higher level, more complex constructs are used. The human has difficulty remembering the intermediate steps to a solution, and indeed, may even not know them. Instead the experts might believe their performance to be based on hunches and intution rather than a lot of compiled memories. The more competent domain experts become, the less able they are to describe the knowledge they use to solve problems.

Also, experts construct lines of reasoning which are plausible to explain what they have done. This reasoning is not necessarily what they did, it is rather a convenient way of representing it. For example, they pretend to do things by the text book, without heuristics or rules of thumb.

This also explains the difference between the rules which the expert states and the rules which the expert uses.

Another problem with knowledge acquisition which will be covered in greater detail later, is the need to elicit the structure of the knowledge as well as the actual knowledge itself.

Finally, there is the problem of representation. Once the knowledge has been elicited, it is necessary to adapt it to the machine and also to keep it in a form which the expert can still refer to and check. This has been one of the claimed advantages of simple expert shells, which require input in the form of if-then rules and which allow the expert to review the form of these rules and amend them easily.

7.3 METHODS OF KNOWLEDGE ACQUISITION

There are many methods of knowledge acquisition. Knowledge may be elicited directly from the expert, through simple questioning in an explicit way, it may be indirectly elicited through observation or through other sources of expertise eg training manuals, or it may be elicited through a combination of many techniques.

Four broad-classes of knowledge acquisition are identified. There is overlap between the areas and one particular technique will rarely be sufficient by itself.

- Text analysis. This is knowledge acquisition without recourse to an expert but through the use of text-books and user manuals.

- Interview analysis. This involves the knowledge engineer in studying verbal protocols, questionnaire responses etc. This provides information directly from the expert.

- Behaviour analysis. This requires the knowledge engineer to make observational studies such as making films of the expert. It is generally not enough just to observe the in-vivo performance of the expert. The expert is generally required to verbalise reasons and provide explanations for decisions either during the task, or when reviewing it at a later date.

- Machine induction. Theoretically, this removes the bottleneck, by replacing knowledge acquisition with the much less arduous task of collecting case history. However, as we shall see later, there are limits to the power of this technique.

7.3.1 Text analysis

This represents one of the least tried methods of constructing an expert system. Its main advantage is that it does not require the knowledge engineer to have direct access to the expert who might represent a valuable and scarce resource.

Text analysis is fraught with difficulties. The knowledge engineer is required to assimilate knowledge in a very difficult way. Few people are good at 'book' learning.

If text analysis is the sole source of information the knowledge engineer will be required to solve dilemmas and problems without reference to an external expert.

The resultant system is less likely to be satisfactory. It will be difficult for the knowledge engineer to evaluate and may not address many of the domain problems.

This particular method of knowledge acquisition is probably the least successful and should be only sparingly used. Text analysis generally requires the knowledge engineer to become an expert in the domain which the expert system is concerned with, and the resultant problems rarely outweigh the gains. Whilst this method might provide the knowledge engineer with an overview, such that it is possible to talk intelligently to the expert, it should be used with caution.

A problem in using text analysis in combination with other techniques is that the knowledge engineer will start to acquire some of the characteristics of the expert without having the necessary understanding of the expertise. This can be best seen when the expert and knowledge engineer are able to use the same language to describe the problem.

If text analysis is used during the early stages of knowledge elicitation, as a route towards 'educating' the knowledge engineer, then the knowledge engineer is able to converse with the expert in jargon which the knowledge engineer thinks means one thing but which the expert is using in a totally different way. This semantic difficulty frequently occurs during the process of knowledge acquisition and can only be dealt with by requiring the expert to explain anything which is doubtful and by following an iterative design process which requires the expert to comment on each rule and system performance.

One area in which text analysis is useful is the development of systems to encapsulate rules and regulations, such as legal advice systems. In these cases knowledge acquisition can be considered in two main areas. The first is the body of knowledge - the rules and regulations. The second is other issues, such as how to apply them, what short cuts are available, and so on. Even when developing these relatively precise systems, text analysis should only be used in tandem with discussions with a human expert. The expert may, for example, be aware of an overall structure encompassing the rules which is not reflected by the text based material.

7.3.2 Interview analysis

Interview analysis is an explicit technique of knowledge acquisition. It requires the knowledge engineer to interact with the expert. Explicit techniques rely on the domain experts telling the knowledge engineer about their knowledge in a comprehensive and understandable way. The simplest method of doing this is to use a questionnaire. Ask the experts about their knowledge. This has several advantages. It is easy to interpret. Provided that the questionnaire has been well designed, it is easy to analyse and to translate the information into terms which the system designer can use. However there are several problems associated with interview analysis. Firstly, the knowledge engineer has to know which questions to ask. This can be especially hard if the knowledge engineer has little knowledge about the expertise.

Secondly, if the questionnaire is too restrictive in the answers it allows, the knowledge engineer can often miss information which is crucial or miss underlying cues which the expert applies when using the expertise.

There are many other problems associated with questionnaire design. For example, the problem of leading questions, the failure to elicit underlying information, the need to ensure that the information supplied is correct and is not just the expert providing the 'correct' or 'book' answer. Techniques for good questionnaire design have been covered in many books, for example Oppenheimer (2) provides detailed guidelines on how to design, apply and analyse questionnaires. Whilst these guidelines are for market researchers and the like, the underlying rules do not change.

The knowledge engineer must decide on the information which is required, as well as deciding how the information is going to be analysed (or in this case, translated into rules for the expert system) prior to applying the questionnaire. The questionnaire must be unambigious and unbiased.

There will still be problems which the knowledge engineer will have to address. One method of avoiding some of these problems is to ask more open ended questions. This produces results which are hard to interpret and require elaboration which might not be available. Questionnaires comprising primarily open-ended questions will generate a lot more data, in a fairly unstructured way. However, ideally such questions should produce data which it is possible to interpret. Also, they should provide details about how the expert actually carries out the task and what the important aspects of the task are, rather than producing results which are for the benefit of the knowledge engineer. Too often users will tailor their performance and resposnes to try to 'please' the knowledge engineer.

A more subtle method of eliciting this type of information is to use unobtrusive questionnaires. Typical of this approach is to use a repertory grid technique. It is worthwhile explaining this technique as it is representative of a method of knowledge acquisition which allows the knowledge engineer to produce information about how the expert thinks and what the priorities and important factors are.

The repertory grid was developed by Kelly in the 1950s (3). The grid was originally envisaged as a pyschiatric tool but has seen wide use in areas such as advertising, demographic studies and group dynamics. The beauty of the technique is that it allows for the probing of peoples' internal 'constructualised' view of the world without the need to explicitly state what that view is. Kelly believed that each individual viewed the world differently and that these differences could be explained in terms of an individual's personal constructs. Having determined these constructs the therapist would be able to view the world through the patient's eyes. Kelly further devised a method of eliciting these constructs.

From this initial work, many methods of construct elicitation have been developed. We will describe one of those techniques.

The basis of the technique is to define an area of interest (in the case of knowledge acquisition this would be some aspect of the expert's knowledge). Once the area of interest has been sufficiently delineated it is described in terms of elements which comprise the domain. This is fairly simple when the psychiatrist is using the technique to consider a disturbed individual's frame of reference, it is less easy when the expert is a complex individual with a complex and sophisticated frame of reference. Typically, the elements chosen to represent the domain should include all aspects which the expert feels are important. Determining these elements involves the knowledge engineer talking to the expert, studying the task and agreeing important aspects of it. This can pose some problems but one of the features of the Grid is that it can reveal gaps in the element set provided that most of the important elements have been used.

Once the domain has been sufficiently described, in terms of its elements, the expert is required to place these elements in his own 'constructualised' view of the world.

A typical way in which the expert's constructs are generated is to present the elements in threes and ask what one characteristic two have in common and the third one doesn't. This is known as triad elicitation and the number of triads presented to the user is a function of element size, and the expert's complexity. Typically, the more constructs the user is able to generate the more complex the world view and the more complete the description. It is important that the individual generates different constructs (though the difference between the constructs becomes explicit when the grid is analysed).

Once a sufficient number of constructs have been generated the user is asked to describe each element in terms of the constructs. Typically, the user is presented with an element list and asked to rate each element in terms of each construct, for example by ranking the elements within a construct, going from the element which is most like the construct to the element which is most like the exact opposite of that construct (**not** least like the construct).

It is important to note that the elements are rated on a bipolar scale within each construct. Bipolarity is a feature of the way in which the constructs are described to the subject.

Based upon the construct which the individual produces, the knowledge engineer must either explicitly determine from the individual what the exact opposite of the construct is or else produce a semantic representation of that opposite pole. A bipolar construct is one which ranges from black to white rather than from black to grey. Whilst it may seem a question of semantics, research has shown that bipolarity will significantly influence an individual's responses. If the grid is to provide a sufficiently accurate view, then the experts must understand that they are rating the elements on a bipolar scale.

When the individual has completed this task, the knowledge engineer is left with the raw material necessary to produce a constructualised view of a specific domain.

The interpretation of repertory grids is difficult and requires much skill and experience. Fortunately many programs have been developed to help with this interpretation, particularly those produced by Gaines & Shaw (4). Typically, the most significant constructs are determined and a series of maps are made, showing the relationship between constructs eg by plotting the relationships the constructs have to the two most significant, but dissimilar constructs. Further information on this technique can be found in Francella & Bannister (5).

Apart from the problems of interpretation repertory grids also suffer from other drawbacks, and furthermore, there are ethical considerations. They are, by nature, extremely intrusive, but not in an obvious manner. Thus individuals might provide information of which they are not aware. The knowledge engineer must be very careful how this information is used and must determine whether or not to feed back the results to the expert. One of the strengths of the grid in psychiatry is that it can be used in a therapeutic way to change as well as understand behaviour, and this might be a serious drawback if used in this way for this application.

Similarly, the knowledge engineer must be very careful in interpreting the grid. Whilst it can be very good at highlighting major areas of concern, provided that the elements have been chosen with sufficient care and are representative of the domain, it is fairly easy to misunderstand the relative importance of individual elements. We have already stated that element choice should be as much as

possible determined by the expert and hopefully fully
reflective of the domain. Should the grid produce anomalous
results it is worthwhile re-investigating the element set.

Whilst the quality of the information gathered through a
repertory grid technique is very high, it is sometimes difficult
to apply the information to the specific expert system
especially as repertory grids deal with feeling and view rather
than facts and specific information.

Howevever, they should be employed as part of a battery of
interview techniques simply because it is virtually impossible
to predict what information they will produce and how
relevant that information will be to the eventual success of the
expert system project.

Another interview technique which is worth exploring is the
use of critical incident analysis. The expert is required to
consider either system failure or critical incident - of the form
'what happens if...' This is a very useful technique for
determining the unusual.

To produce information about the expert's normal problems
and tasks, something like the day-in-the-life of scenario (as
reported in (6)) can be used. This can be a very useful
technique, as it is less time consuming than making the user
keep a diary but provides a similar type of information, with
the user required to produce a more or less detailed plan of a
typical day.

In taking either of these approaches it is important to look
not only at critical incident, but also at temporal variance -
how does the task fluctuate on a week to week, year to year,
etc., basis.

Another technique for eliciting task specific information
has been developed by the HUSAT research group, from
original work done by the Royal Navy. This is known as PTR -
Personalised Task Representation technique. PTR requires the
individual to follow an action diagram procedure. Each part of
the task is represented in diagrammatic form with specific
inputs and outputs and the interviewer asks questions such as
'Why do this' or 'How is this achieved'.

Crucial in all these interview techniques is the role of the interviewer who is required to follow up and clarify as well as record.

Nearly all interview techniques, bar the most structured and constrained, will require the interviewer to adopt a positive role and to interact with the expert. This can cause problems, especially when the knowledge engineer notes information which is clear at the time but becomes less obvious in retrospect.

There are several other techniques for interview analysis, based along lines already discussed. The three presented below are taken from (7):

- Problem discussion: explore the kinds of data, knowledge, and procedures needed to solve specific problems.

- Problem description: have the expert describe a prototypical problem for each category of answer in the domain.

- Problem analysis: present the expert with a series of realistic problems to solve aloud, probing the rationale behind the reasoning steps.

To adequately use the above three techniques the knowledge engineer must be able to structure information in a reasonable form and conduct useful, highly interactive conversations.

The advantage of concentrating on specific problems is that specific information can be obtained. The disadvantage is that the knowledge engineer might miss key problems or mis-interpret the results.

This disadvantage leads to consideration of the next stage in interview analysis, which is the feedback process.

Once the expert has provided the basic information and rules the knowledge engineer should aim to improve the knowledge. This is a three stage process:

- System refinement: have the expert give you a series of problems to solve using the rules acquired from the interviews.

- System examination: have the expert examine and critique the prototype system's rules and control structure.

- System validation: present the cases solved by the expert and prototype system to other outside experts.

This will provide the knowledge engineer with the necessary feedback to assess whether the expert system is meeting the experts' requirements and representing their expertise.

It is worth noting that where several experts are available, it may be helpful to organise feedback sessions with experts other than those interviewed. Such experts will naturally have less personal commitment to justifying the original interview, and will be available to take a more objective stance. However, such meetings can also cause problems, particularly in cases where the different approaches of experts are not so much right and wrong, but more a 'question of style'.

7.3.3 Behaviour analysis

Apart from interviewing the expert, the knowledge engineer can also observe. Observation techniques come in many forms. Some are based on methodologies developed for time and motion studies some 50 years ago. These involve breaking down the expert's behaviour mechanistically and studying each small movement. Others are more holistic, such as videoing an expert and then determining expertise from observation. For example, Charles Church (formerly of British Telecom) has used a hi-tech interview with the expert working on the task, talking into a microphone and being video recorded, with perhaps the interviewer annotating the proceedings. (this experiment has been recorded in the Alvey video – 'Expert systems in British industry', available from the National Computer Centre).

The advantage of such a technique is that it doesn't miss anything. It captures the expert performing the task and may be reviewed, in part, in slow motion or in other ways at the interviewer's leisure. It does not require the expert to repeat the same task many times. The knowledge engineer can examine discrete areas and compare what the expert says with what is done. The amount of expert time used is kept to a minimum.

The disadvantages are that the technique is obtrusive and may be intimidating. The expert might not behave in a natural manner. Also, the technique generates a lot of data, with perhaps a 10:1 analysis time to recorded time ratio. This can mean the knowledge engineer becomes bogged down and overwhelmed with information which is of little or no importance.

Observation of the expert provides a quality of data which can not be gained in any other way. It provides at least one example of how the expert can apply knowlege to carry out a task.

As with the interview techniques it may only capture one small aspect and might not deal with critical incidents or with tasks which vary with time or circumstances.

7.3.4 Machine induction

Since the early days of artificial intelligence research, one of the long term goals has been the construction of computer systems capable of learning. Clearly, a fully competent learning computer would solve the problems of knowledge acquisition at a stroke. So far, few practical results have come from this area of research. One area where progress has been made, and some practical benefits are being claimed, is in machine induction.

The major premise of the approach is that many expert tasks or sub-tasks come down to a classification problem (some examples are shown in fig 7.1). The aim of machine induction is to induce a general rule which covers all cases from a sample of example cases. Fig 7.2 shows a typical example of this process.

A number of mathematical techniques have been devised to generate efficient decision trees (that is, with questions arranged in such a way as to minimise the number of questions that must be asked before a classification is reached). Perhaps the best known is Quinlan's ID3 algorithm.

Which illness does this patient have ?

Which pension scheme best suits this client ?

Which semiconductor provides the required performance ?

Which techniques are appropriate to the statistical analysis of this data ?

Fig 7.1 Classification problems

Child	Temp	Red Spots	Measles (yes/no)
Henry	106	Yes	Yes
Tom	103	No	No
Jane	101	No	No
Alison	98	Yes	No
Andrew	104	Yes	Yes

From this data, one can induce the rule that;

'if a child has red spots and a temperature greater than 103°
then the child has measles'

Fig 7.2   Simple induction

Commercial implementations of this are available, notably from the Turing Institute (which is headed by Donald Michie, one of induction's foremost proponents).

The most obvious limitation of the technique is that it allows only the development of classification rules. However this may not be quite the limitation it seems at first sight - many tasks can be rephrased as classification exercises, or perhaps split into simpler sub-tasks which fall into the classification category.

More subtly, the system requires a relevant and complete set of criteria. In the example of fig 7.2, a different set of criteria (for example, colour of eyes, rather than temperature and red spots) might have coincidentally generated a rule which gave the correct example for each of the sample cases. Two solutions exist to this problem:

- turn to the expert to identify the important factors. Although this smacks of 'doing the knowledge acquisition anyway', it is much easier for an expert to simply list the important factors rather than attempt to explain their interrelationships

- a 'sufficient' set of examples must be input to the induction process. This is a crucial requirement. Sufficiency in this context is not clearly definable. Only post-hoc studies will reveal what the minimum set would have been. Clearly, extremes must be represented, as well as borderline cases and those which lie on either side. Knowledge about these narrow decisions is precisely that which is difficult to elicit conventionally, and induction must allow it to be obtained to be a fully worthwhile technique.

Particular problems are caused by continuous variables. An example is described by Bloomfield (7). The problem is to induce a rule to identify graph points which are on the line $x = y$. The obvious training set is a group of points, some of which are on the line.

Bloomfield used the training set shown in fig 7.3, and used the 'Expert-Ease' induction package to induce the rules shown in fig 7.4. Clearly the rule is **wrong** (although trying to explain exactly why gives an insight into many of the problems of knowledge elicitation), and the problem is that to arrive at the correct rule from the sample set it is not enough to simply compare the sets of attributes of the different example points. Rather, it is necessary to consider the relationships between

x	y	On line ?
1	0	No
0	1	No
1	1	Yes
2	1	No
3	3	Yes
5	1	No
6	6	Yes
6	7	No
8	9	No
10	10	Yes

Fig 7.3   Training Set for $x = y$ (Bloomfield (7))

the attributes (in this case, the x and y coordinates), and apply some general knowledge of the domain (graphs).

Finally, the set of examples may need to be 'sanitised'. The exceptions to the rule (for example, the child whose body temperature is normal and yet does have measles) must be removed. Often the presence of such examples may be revealed by inconsistencies in the decision tree, but one cannot rely upon this.

The need to select a good example set is thus the biggest problem. A lot depends upon the consequences of an error: if these are not too critical, than one can effectively allow the system to 'learn on the job'. Each time an incorrect classification is made, a new example can be added to the set, ensuring that the mistake is not repeated.

Problems in question ordering may also occur if an inflexible induction package is being used. For example, consider a system we designed to diagnose faults in TV sets. The induction system picked the best question to ask first purely in terms of minimising the number of questions required

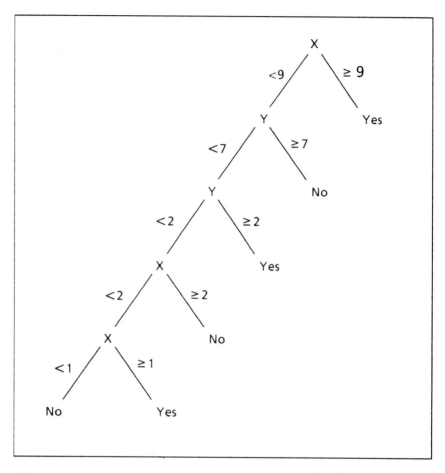

Fig 7.4   An induced decision procedure for $X = Y$ (Bloomfield (7))

to reach a diagnosis. This question related to a component buried inside the set. This approach is in marked contrast to that of a TV engineer, who starts by answering all the questions that relate to the external state of the TV. Once again, the system has been let down by its lack of general knowledge about the domain, rather than knowledge directly related to the classification problem at hand.

The poor ordering of questions is symptomatic of a more general fault with induction - the system does not solve problems in the same way as the expert. It will not adopt different strategies according to circumstances. Furthermore, the unnatural rules generated by the system will not make it easy to supply meaningful explanations to the user.

To sum up, there are a number of potential problems in the use of induction. However, it is undoubtedly useful in some cases; for example, diagnosing clearly defined faults in equipment. Commercial successes involving millions of dollars have been reported by, for example, the Westinghouse Corporation. The best advice that can be offered is to consider whether any of the above problems may arise, and if not, then machine induction is likely to be at the least a valuable adjunct to the knowledge acquisition process.

One unique advantage of machine induction is that it does offer the possibility of deducing new knowledge. It may be possible to list all the factors which influence a decision, without understanding their impacts, and to induce a rule which works successfully. The technique should certainly be considered where there are plentiful test data and a well-defined classification problem to solve.

7.4 SOME PROBLEMS WITH KNOWLEDGE ELICITATION

Often the knowledge engineer needs to consult several experts about the same task. This raises several problems. Often the experts seem to produce data which are contradictory. This can lead to the knowledge engineer becoming an expert in conflict resolution.

For example, consider the case of an expert system used to determine which is the best database for a micro-computer. One expert, to the question: 'What is the best database for this application' replies 'Package A', another expert replies 'Package B'.

The knowledge engineer determines what criteria the experts used to come to this conclusion and finds that they are the same. It then becomes necessary to test the two databases or to consult a third expert. There does not seem to be a best way of dealing with conflicting information, unless one piece of information is definitely 'wrong' and this can easily be determined. A feature of experts is that they often disagree and the knowledge engineer is forced to make compromises. In such cases the knowledge engineer must be practical, adopting the approach which works.

Sometimes conflicting information is the result of ambiguity in the data. This must be resolved by following up the problem and determining the reason why the ambiguity/conflict occurs.

Another problem with knowledge acquisition is the expert's perception of the value of the expert system. If the expert feels threatened or exposed by the process of building the expert system then the knowledge engineer is unlikely to be successful. One of the keys to success is to have the full co-operation of both management and experts.

It is unlikely that the expert system will serve to replace experts, rather it will relieve them of burdensome, trivial tasks and free their time for more important, challenging problems.

Generally the term expert system is a misnomer and the expert system is used to provide guidance rather than expertise. It is important that the expert recognises this and sees the system as an aid rather than as a threat.

When the expert system is intended to replace the expert it becomes more difficult to persuade the expert to co-operate unless the expert is retiring or changing jobs. Fortunately we are not yet in a position where most expert systems are for replacing rather than aiding experts. Once expert systems start to challenge this basic premise then expert co-operation might become more difficult to obtain.

Another major problem with knowledge acquisition is translating the elicited knowledge into rules which can be input into the expert system.

This problem tends to be dependent upon the form of knowledge which the system will take. For example, some expert shells require the builder to input knowledge in the form of if-then rules and facts. Other systems will induce rules from examples of the knowledge. More complex systems offer other forms of knowledge representation.

The problem of getting the knowledge in the right form is further complicated by the need to feedback to the expert information on what knowledge has been determined as well as informing the less experienced user on what knowledge is being used.

One of the most powerful features of an expert system is that it allows the expert to review the knowledge contained in it, and therefore this knowledge should be in an easily understandable form. This highlights another major requirement of all knowledge acquisition. The process must be iterative. It is not enough for the knowledge engineer to translate the expert's knowledge and for a system to be built. The expert must review the system and point out any failing or refinements which are required.

Even when the expert is satisfied the system must be presented to the user for comment and to test whether it is understandable. A system which the expert can use is satisfactory only if the expert is representative of the ultimate end-users.

Often experts are unaware of how opaque their knowledge is and there is a danger that as the knowledge engineer becomes more involved with the problem, some of this mental block will be passed on.

The only way to check whether the knowledge is in a suitable form for the end-user is to involve the end-user with the system. This should ensure that the knowledge base is not only complete but also useable.

7.5 ATTEMPTS TO SOLVE THE PROBLEM OF KNOWLEDGE ACQUISITION

One of main attempts to solve the problems associated with Knowledge acquisition is to adopt a structured approach. Berry and Broadbent (8) report that:

> 'Companies such as Scicon and the Knowledge Based Systems Centre stress the need to develop a formal specification. This involves looking at the structure of the task involved, the functional class of activity and the user requirement.'

One of the claimed advantages of this approach is that it allows the knowledge engineer to deal with much larger knowledge bases.

This approach also looks at the 'meta-level' knowledge acquisition problem - the structure within which the knowledge lies. We have already stressed the need to determine this structure and the comparative ease of fitting knowledge within this structure. The problem is that there appears to be no easy way of determining this structure. Whilst developing a formal specification is an excellent idea there is as yet no fixed method of doing this.

Another solution is to constrain the domain under consideration. For example consider fault diagnosis rather than user modelling. This lessens many of the problems associated with knowledge acquisition but restricts the applications.

A further approach, which has been adopted in an STC-led Esprit project, is to connect 'raw' (English) expressions of knowledge through a number of intermediate representations into some standard which can be mapped onto the particular implementation vehicle in use. This is clearly redolent of approaches such as SSADM and other structured design methodologies.

The most successful expert systems have not used any one approach to knowledge acquisition. Some have required the expert to serve as knowledge engineer, others have required the knowledge engineer to serve as system builder. The only approach which they all have in common is to redesign the system in the light of experience and to adopt a knowledge acquisition technique most appropriate to the particular domain.

7.6 CONCLUSIONS

Knowledge acquisition has been successfully employed, but despite the conclusions reached by Berry and Broadbent (8) that knowledge acquisition is not a major bottleneck, it still seems to pose significant problems.

These are associated with the need to adopt a multitude of approaches, with, as yet, no one approach offering an ideal solution to every problem.

Probably the most important stage in the knowledge acquisition process is to identify what type of knowledge is required from the expert. This will be used to determine which techniques will be the most appropriate. It is important to employ several techniques, looking at different aspects of the task, and to develop some explicit, formal structure within which the knowledge lies at an early stage.

We have described several techniques of which the knowledge engineer should be aware and we believe that it is particularly important for the knowledge engineer to consider the role of techniques which determines knowledge in an implicit, unobtrusive way. The repertory grid technique has yet to be fully exploited for expert systems but offers a useful way of gaining an insight into the expert's frame of reference.

It is hard to accurately assess the financial costs of the various techniques described in this chapter, or to reccomend one particular approach to knowledge elicitation. The aim of the chapter has been to describe the techniques that are available. The sheer complexity of the domain within which the system is to operate does not necessarily determine the likely cost of the elicitation process. More important factors are the number of experts, their articulateness, and the extent to which the 'rules of the game' are constant from one occasion to the next. Also note that in many cases by far and away the largest cost is the use of the expert's time.

In general, use a range of techniques (or at least two!). Remember that the subjective nature of most approaches will render the system's performance sensitive to the knowledge and approach of the knowledge engineer, and to the personal relationship between knowledge engineer and expert. A competent knowledge engineer who gets on with the expert is likely to be more effective than the greatest AI specialist in the world, if that specialist cannot work with the expert in harmony.

We will now explore some practical expert system projects by considering three case studies. These represent actual projects, undertaken to implement IKBSs into organisations.

7.7 REFERENCES

1. Rylko H M, (1985) 'Artificial Intelligence: Bibliographic summaries of selected literature,' The Report Store

2. Oppenheimer A N, (1966) 'Questionnaire Design: Attitude Measurement,' Heinemann

3. Kelly G A, (1955) 'The psychology of personal constructs,' vols 1 & 2 Norton NY

4. Gaines B R & Shaw M L G, (1980) 'New directions in the analysis and interactive elicitation of personal construct systems,' International Journal of Man-machine studies 1980, 13, 81-116

5. Francella F & Bannister D, (1977) 'A manual for repertory grid technique,' Academic Press

6. Macaulay L & Hutt A, (1986) 'User skills and task match methodology workshop,' Human Factors in product specification, York, ICL & Huddersfield Polytechnic.

7. Bloomfield BP, (1986) 'Capturing expertise by rule induction,' Knowledge Engineering Review, Vol 1 No 4

8. Berry D C & Broadbent D E, (1986) 'Expert systems and man-machine interface,' Expert Systems, 3, 4, pp 228-231

8

Case studies

8.1 INTRODUCTION

The aim of this chapter is to present three expert systems which have been constructed, and to consider ways in which they demonstrate good and bad practice from a human factors standpoint. The systems selected are all very different, in terms of cost, environment, expected users, the hardware and software tools used, and the benefits to be gained from their use. Fig 8.1 summarises these aspects of the differing systems.

As might be expected with such a diverse range of applications, direct comparisons are not of much benefit. Instead, we attempt to show the limit and potential of different approaches to expert system building.

8.2 ESCORT - EXPERT SYSTEM FOR COMPLEX OPERATIONS IN REAL TIME

Author's note: much of the discussion of the interfaces of ESCORT relates to unpublished work. However, constant reference is made in other areas to various attributes of the

System	Escort	DES Pensions	RAF Stores
Cost	High	Medium	Low
Environment	Process plant control room	Office	Office
Task	Process plant control - avoiding shutdown	Answering queries about pensions	Fault diagnosis on computers
Users	Process plant operators & engineers- little computer knowledge	Clerical staff - no technical knowledge	Computer specialists
H/W and S/W	Lisp machine, toolkit & Lisp, touch sensitive screen for operators	Mainframe & shell	PC and shell
Benefits	Financial gain from better quality output and less downtime	Faster, more consistent & correct answers; evaluation of policy decisions	Coping with loss of skilled staff

Fig 8.1   Comparison of three applications

ESCORT system.   References 4, 5 and 6 cover, respectively,
the requirements, the overall structure of ESCORT, and the
causal reasoning aspects in more detail.

8.2.1 The problem

The control and management of process control plants has been an area of continual development for many years. Instrumentation has developed from manual to automatic, from analogue to digital, and from local to centralised operation. From the point of view of individual process control operators, perhaps the largest effect has been in the amount of information they have available on which to base their decisions. There are a number of factors which contribute to this. Firstly, computerised, digital techniques make it possible to offer the operator access to a wider range of information: secondly, larger installations are being built and controlled from a single nerve centre: and thirdly, there has been demand for increased information from management.

An indication of the potential size of the problem is given by the Three Mile Island nuclear plant. This had 2000 alarms, and a similar array of analogue displays. This large amount of information sources is not the end of the story. In one simulated incident, 500 lights went on or off in the first minute, and 800 in the second (1). Thus the problem for operators is a combination of very large quantities of information coupled with an environment in which things can change rapidly.

In such a situation, humans suffer from 'cognitive overload'. Cognitive overload occurs when operators are faced with situations which are too complex and changing too rapidly for the human to be able to follow and understand everything that happens.

Fitts claimed that humans do at least deteriorate gracefully in such a situation (2). However, this is small consolation when the relevant information that could avert disaster is contained in a few amongst several hundred displays. Whilst the operator will not stop working effectively, it is likely that the correct course of action will not always be found in time.

Another feature of cognitive overload is a general falling off in response time. Even when the operator is required to solve simple problems, or perform simple motor tasks, the time taken for each operation is increased.

The reverse of cognitive overload - cognitive underload - has been less well studied in such situations. However, it appears that an operator with very little stimulation also experiences a dropping off in performance. Simple studies of arousal indicate that there is an optimum level of stress at which an operator performs best.

Studies such as those carried out by at the Royal Dutch Stel Plant at Hoogovens (3) indicate that if an operator is under-aroused, skill deteriorates and the operator is less inclined to act, more prone to letting the computer sort things out, until the problem has reached a stage where neither operator nor computer can save the day. The New Scientist (3) reports

'The operators became so unsure of themselves that, or some occasions, they actually left the pulpit used for control unmanned...(and they) also failed fully to understand the control theory of the programs ... and this reinforced their attitude of 'standing well back' from the operation - except when things were going very awry. By intervening late, the operators let the productivity drop below that of plant using traditional control methods.'

To sum up, process plant control has become such a complex business that operators can suffer cognitive overload. In the worst case, the effect may be total plant shutdown, caused by the failure of operators to spot serious faults amongst a morass of information in time for preventative action to be effective. Such shutdowns are an extremely costly business.

8.2.2 The requirement

Complex process control rooms may have 20000+ alarms. It is certain that at any one time a proportion of these will be on; no process plant of this size is likely to be functioning perfectly throughout at any one time. The operator has three problems when a new alarm occurs. Firstly, is this a symptom of a previously noted problem ? Secondly, if not, then what is the new problem underlying this alarm ? Thirdly, does the new event impact the operator's view of which problems should be attended to first ? In this context, it is worth remarking that most problems will cause a number of alarms - one consequence of the large amount of information displayed to the operators.

These three tasks must be carried out in real time, so an effective operator should anticipate crises.

ESCORT (Expert system for complex operations in real time) was designed by PA Computer & Telecommunications to support the operator addressing these problems.

8.2.3 Interface requirements

The operator's interface needs above all to be simple and concise. Whilst this is generally true of all interfaces, it is of particular importance where the problem is cognitive overload. For example, the operator should be able to see as much or as little information as required at any one time, whether at the macro, overall system level, or at the micro, individual problem level.

Additionally, it is considered important that ESCORT should not dominate. As mentioned earlier, the perils of cognitive underload are every bit as real as those of overload. Operators can become either deskilled (forgetting their own knowledge) or uninterested (carrying out advice without pausing to evaluate its true worth).

Apart from the operator's interface, the system requires an 'Engineer's interface ' to enable a process engineer to modify the system's knowledge. There are several aspects to this knowledge. Space does not permit a detailed description of this interface.

This interface to the knowledge base needs to use terms which the user understands (the user will be a process plant engineer, not a computer programmer). It must be easy to use, and particularly, easy to relearn (it will only be used occasionally after the initial commissioning period).

8.2.4 The ESCORT system

As ESCORT operates as an expert system in a process control problem it has to operate in real time. In this context, real time is seen as under 1 second. This level of performance is achieved by breaking down the overall problem into a four stage pipeline, and providing a scheduler to supervise the progress of various items along this pipeline.

Both this scheduler and the four elements in the pipeline are knowledge-based systems (KBSs): thus ESCORT comprises five knowledge-based systems. The structure is shown in fig 8.2.

Working from top to bottom through the pipeline, the first KBS detects 'significant events', or departures from desired operation. A simple example is an alarm occurring.

These significant events are then prioritised. Because at this stage the underlying problems are unknown, prioritisation is neccesarily crude (for example, a high pressure alarm on some vessel may receive a high priority, when in reality the underlying problem (an alarm circuit has failed) is relatively unimportant).

The third and largest KBS is the Main Diagnostic System. Its two principal functions are to link events and the underlying problems that caused them to occur. The operation of this module is discussed in more detail below.

Finally, the underlying problems are prioritised. This prioritisation may reverse the decisions of the event prioritisation in the light of the actual cause of an event.

The use of a knowledge-based scheduler enables these tasks to be addressed in an order which allows ESCORT to respond flexibly to the signals from the process plant. Thus, for example, if a new event of very high priority is detected amid a number of minor faults, ESCORT can 'drop everything' and concentrate on this new problem. The scheduler regards servicing operator requests for information as a high priority task.

Apart from the five knowledge-based systems, fig 8.2 also introduces a module which controls the operator's interface (but is not knowledge-based).

8.2.5 The operator's interface

The operator's interface is shown in fig 8.3. It is implemented

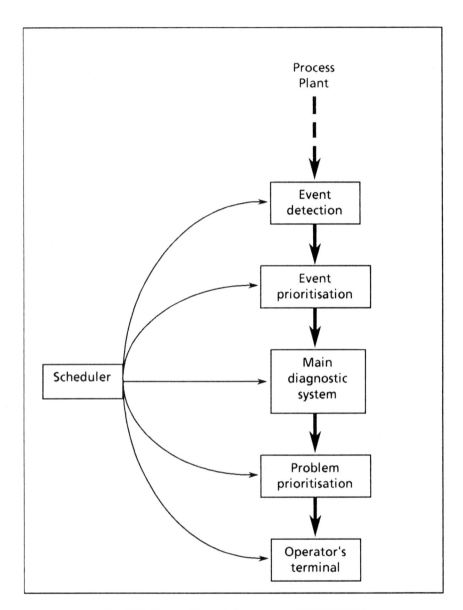

Fig 8.2 Overall architecture of ESCORT

on a colour touch sensitive screen. Down the right hand side is a 'priority ladder' which reflects the output of the problem prioritisation KBS. Higher priority alarms are at the top of the ladder: the six most important are displayed at any one time. This ladder is a dynamic display – both the items on it and their

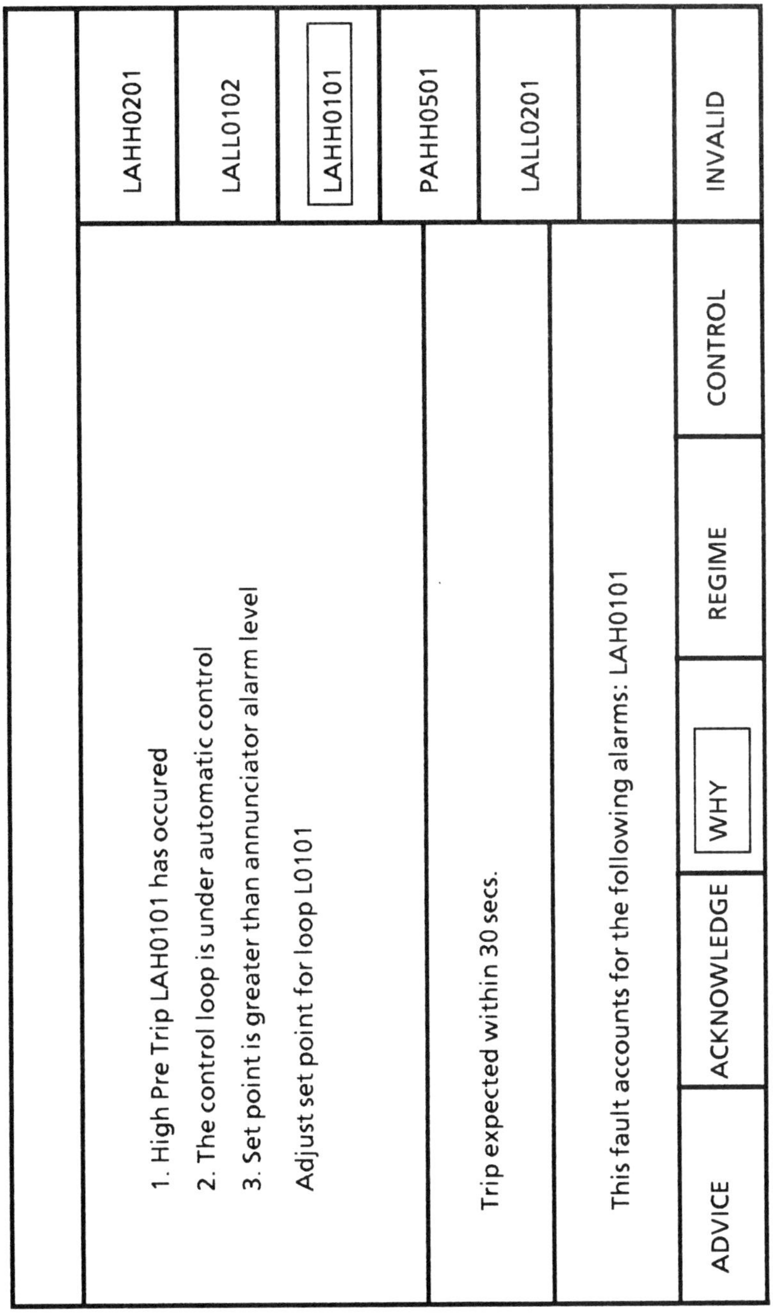

1. High Pre Trip LAH0101 has occured		LAHH0201
2. The control loop is under automatic control		LALL0102
3. Set point is greater than annunciator alarm level		LAHH0101
Adjust set point for loop L0101		PAHH0501
		LALL0201
Trip expected within 30 secs.		
This fault accounts for the following alarms: LAH0101		INVALID
ADVICE	ACKNOWLEDGE	WHY	REGIME	CONTROL

Figure 8.3   Operator's Touch Sensitive Screen in "WHY" Mode

ordering will change over time. Each ladder entry is touch sensitive, and touching a given entry results in the relevant advice being displayed in the centre of the the screen. This central area is divided into three regions: the top region describes the problem, the middle one the estimated time to any possible shutdown, and the bottom region lists any other alarms which have also been caused by the problem being displayed.

Thus the operator has the freedom to inspect any problem, not just the one which the system regards as having currently the highest priority. In order that the operator should not ignore important problems, there is a status bar across the top of the screen. When there are no outstanding problems this is green: when the most significant problem is unlikely to cause a shutdown, it is yellow: and when failure to attend to the most significant problem will cause a failure, it is red.

Finally, a row of touch sensitive buttons across the bottom of the screen provide access to other command options. Those used on an everyday basis include:

Why -   To get an explanation of the chain of reasoning which led the system to link this problem with a particular significant event

Advice -   To return to the default display of the problem description

Acknowledge -   To let ESCORT know its diagnosis has been noted. This allows the problem prioritiser to adjust the priority of a problem in the knowledge that some corrective action should be being taken. If, however, the problem persists, then the priority will gradually rise to its former level. Acknowledged problems are colour coded, so that an operator can tell at a glance which problems have yet to be attended to.

The other buttons can be used to adjust ESCORT's strategy, or to indicate to ESCORT which items of instrumentation are perhaps faulty.

8.2.6 ESCORT's operator interface - a critique

The operator's interface is central to the ESCORT system. The development of ESCORT's overall architecture was influenced by a conception of the user requirements. For example, the motivation for the problem prioritisation KBS was driven largely by the need to help the operator concentrate on just the most important problems, hence reducing the cognitive overload effect. The priority ladder is perhaps the central feature of the operator's interface. The number of items on the ladder, coupled with the importance of the topmost item (shown by the status bar) gives a very quick, crude overview of the plant's current state.

The separation of the priority ladder and status bar from the advice region enables the system to continually update its displays in real time, without distracting the user from the problem currently forming the focus of attention. At the same time, the status bar can provide a crude form of interrupt - if this turns red then a highly important change to the plant's status has occurred.

These then, are the means by which ESCORT seeks to provide real time response, and yet minimise the increase in the cognitive load on its users. A touch sensitive screen was chosen in an attempt to decrease the training - especially for process control operators with minimal computer experience and poor keyboard skills. It has the further advantage that it removes the very real possibility that operators may forget codes in times of stress.

The interface should also be designed to encourage operator autonomy, so that they do not abdicate responsibility to the computer. As mentioned earlier, the priority ladder forms the hub of the interaction. Although this allows the operator access to information regarding each of the problems, it still requires the operator to form an overall plan for dealing with the situation. This will include several decisions, including which problem to deal with first, when to acknowledge a problem, and when to ignore either a problem or ESCORT's advice. It is hoped that the need to do this will force the operators to retain most of their skills. Also of relevance here is the quality of response from the 'Why' button. If the explanations are relevant and easily understood, the operators will be more likely to read them, and then be able to challenge them.

Overall, the interface is designed with process control operators in mind. The use of cues, colour coding, clear displays and the use of touch as the primary input method should help minimise errors.

In order to understand the problems of providing the explanations mentioned above, it is necessary to understand how ESCORT links cause and effect, or in other words what goes on inside the Main Diagnostic System.

8.2.7 Diagnostic knowledge and reasoning in ESCORT

The approach to reasoning in ESCORT was selected with a number of goals in mind. In particular:

- to link problems with their effects (remembering that for each problem there may potentially be many distinct effects)

- to reason in real time

- to reason along lengthy chains, both across a plant and through time.

These objectives are met by the use of 'causal knowledge.' In essence, ESCORT's knowledge about process plants is composed of simple statements describing very local cause/effect relationships within the plant (hence 'causal').

Each of these cause/effect relationships is known as a causal coupling. An example, phrased in English, might be:

'A possible cause for a high level of liquid inside a vessel is an abnormally low flow of liquid in an output pipe.'

The tasks of the main diagnostic system within ESCORT are manyfold, but essentially it must join couplings together to form a chain which links the observed undesirable symptoms (primary events) with causes which the operator can take some action to rectify. To this end, it must link the couplings together, attempt to assess the extent to which they reflect the actual state of the plant, choose between alternatives, and other actions which can be lumped together under the banner of 'reasoning'. This requires a great deal of knowledge which is additional to the simple couplings described above, but this is not described here.

Another way to view a causal coupling is as a statement which links two hypotheses about the process plant. In the example above, these are:

'The level of liquid is high'
'The flow in the pipe is low'

Thus a coupling can be viewed as a set of potential (potential because only true on some occasions) links between pairs of hypotheses. Thus the couplings can be used to construct a network in which the nodes are hypotheses, and the links are couplings.

An example of such a network is shown in fig 8.4. We will refer to this example in the following description of the operation of the main diagnostic system.

In its role as an analyser of the underlying causes for some significant event (detected by the significant event detector), the Main diagnostic system can use the couplings to create a chain of reasoning leading from the significant event (represented as a hypothesis about the process plant) to the causes of that event. In the case of fig 8.4, the significant event is that 'the status of PAL0101 is on' (PAL0101 is a low pressure alarm) and the underlying cause is 'the position of RV01 is open' (RV01 is a safety valve).

In order to pick a path through the network of potential hypotheses and couplings which links a significant event to its causes, ESCORT needs to come to conclusions about the causal strength of hypotheses. In other words, ESCORT must assess the likelihood that a particular hypothesis is true, and makes a contribution to the chain of reasoning under investigation. Evaluation of the truth of hypotheses enables ESCORT to discard chains of reasoning which do not map onto the reality of the current situation in the process plant, and to settle on the line of reasoning which links a significant event to its most likely underlying cause.

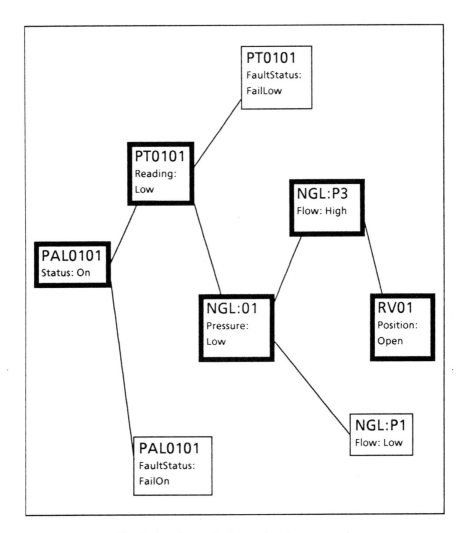

Fig 8.4   Sample hypothesis network

Some hypotheses can be directly tested. An example in fig 8.4 is 'the reading of pressure meter PT0101 is low'. In order to reach conclusions about other hypotheses which cannot be directly measured (eg. 'the pressure of vessel VX01 is low') one must use the results of tests that can be carried out to draw conclusions about other hypotheses. To do this, ESCORT makes use of metarules such as 'if a hypothesis is known to be true then at least one of its causes must also be true' (which effectively makes the assumption that the set of couplings is complete). Thus in the case of fig 8.4, the knowledge (through testing) that the reading of PT0101 was low, and that it had not failed low, combined to show that the pressure of NGL:01 was actually low.

Thus ESCORT can construct networks of hypotheses, and associate a measure of causal strength with each hypothesis. We have said that the levels of causal strength of some hypotheses can be measured, and that these measures of causal strength can be propagated to neighbouring hypotheses. These levels of causal strength are in the range 0-1. The diagnostic task is complete when the network of hypotheses contains a chain which links the significant event being investigated with an underlying cause, and the causal strength values of the hypotheses on that link are high enough for that chain to be regarded as a plausible explanation of the situation in the process plant.

8.2.8 Explaining chains of reasoning

In Chapter 6 we discussed the occasion when a simple transcript of the chain of reasoning employed by an expert system might prove to be too detailed. ESCORT is an example of such a system. In the case of fig 8.4, for example, one might say:

'The status of PAL0101 is known to be On now, because it was tested. PAL0101 being On is caused by the reading of PT0101 being low now, which is known to be the case because it was tested. It has also been tested to show that it is recovering. The reading of PT0101 is low now because the pressure of NGL:01 is low now. The pressure of NGL:01 has been proven to be low because it is the only possible cause for the reading of PT0101 being low, (the alternative cause, that PT0101 had failed low, was discarded because it was tested and found not to be the case). The pressure of NGL:01 is known to be recovering because the reading of PT0101 is known to be recovering. The pressure of NGL:01 is low because the flow of pipe 3 was high (the past status of the flow of pipe 3 can affect the current status of the pressure of NGL:01 because the pressure of NGL:01 is recovering and this coupling is known to have a delayed effect). The flow of pipe 3 was high because the position of RV01 was open. The position of RV01 is known to have been open, because it was tested.'

Such an explanation is unlikely to hold the attention of any operator, let alone that of one suffering from cognitive overload. A more useful interface might say:

'PAL0101 is On because the pressure of NGL:01 is low. This low pressure was caused by RV01 being opened. No action is necessary because RV01 has since been closed, and the pressure of NGL:01 is recovering.'

Chapter 6 describes a number of the problems which make it difficult to extract a useful explanation from a chain of reasoning founded on production rules. The cause-effect chain that ESCORT develops is somewhat analogous to such chains, and it is worth noting the way in which some of these problems do affect ESCORT.

At the time of writing, the ESCORT explanation facility is still under development. Certain things are apparent:

(i) the causal couplings tend to make smaller conceptual leaps than humans. Consider this example of ESCORT's reasoning:

'High level in vessel **because**
High flow in pipe **because**
High flow of liquid X in pipe'

An explanation presented to the operator should normally omit the middle step in this chain. One approach under consideration is to report hypotheses which occur at points where the hypothesis network branches substantially. This has the appeal of both simplicity and reasonableness. It seems a reasonable heuristic, because the interesting part about a particular chain of reasoning is the choice of route through the network of hypotheses. In the example above, the middle hypothesis has only one possible cause (the only possible cause of high flow in a pipe is high flow of one of the substances which the pipe contains) and would thus not be reported under such a regime.

(ii) ESCORT uses certain metarules in constructing a chain of reasoning. As we have suggested above, the most interesting thing about a particular chain of reasoning is the choice of direction through the network of possible hypotheses. In some cases it is easy to explain the choice - a particular hypothesis

has been tested. In others, ESCORT may have used a heuristic
such as:

> 'Everything has a cause, so if all potential cause
> hypotheses but one have been shown to be false, the one
> that remains must be true.'

In order to provide full explanations, ESCORT therefore needs
to keep track of how it derived the preferred explanation of
the problems the operator is facing.

8.2.9 ESCORT - the future

ESCORT is currently undergoing further development. To
assess fully the effectiveness of the interface further steps
will need to be taken.

It will be important to monitor the types of errors which
are made by operators of the system. The system is intended
for use in a critical area, and it is therefore of the utmost
importance that the system gain the operators' confidence at
an early stage. The operator's interface must therefore allow
for operators to gain sufficient understanding of the system to
build that confidence.

Finally, the two interfaces (to engineers and operators) are
very different. This is as it should be, because the two user
classes have very different tasks when they approach the
machine. Nevertheless, it is important that the two groups
have a common basis of understanding of the system, and thus
the two interfaces should not present differing pictures of the
underlying expert systems. It is not sufficient to simply avoid
creating misconceptions; one should also aim to give the users
similar views of less clear-cut issues, such as the relative
importance of the various system components.

8.3 AN EXPERT SYSTEM FOR THE DEPARTMENT OF EDUCATION AND SCIENCE

8.3.1 Background

The Department of Education and Science (DES) initiated a project in June 1983 to develop an expert system to aid in the administration of the Teachers' Superannuation Scheme (TSS).

There were several problems associated with the administration of the Scheme. These included:

- the need to formulate consistent decisions such that all similar cases yield the same results

- individual staff working on the TSS often become experts in specific areas. They are used as a source by other members of staff. Their loss can lead to significant gaps in knowledge

- the DES has no easy way of accessing a permanent, up-to-date source of information on the regulations. Consequently, each major revision or consolidation exercise must be accompanied by an extensive historical search

- it is not possible to use the TSS data as a prediction tool to assess the effects of changes imposed by external factors, such as alterations to the state pension scheme.

The TSS is administered by some 290 staff and affects approximately 900,000 teachers, of whom some 550,000 are currently in service.

There are 98 separate regulations and 11 schedules plus 8 sets of amending regulations relating to the TSS, with two or more amendments still in the pipeline.

The staff deal with a range of enquiries from ad-hoc telephone conversations to the provision of policy advice to ministers.

The system has been computerised over 17 years. A mainframe serves as a datastore, with batch facilities to update and retrieve teachers' records, and some limited computational facilities.

The aim of the expert system project was to establish whether the TSS was an appropriate application for an expert system, to identify suitable hardware and software, to determine which sub-section of the TSS could be used as the basis of a pilot system and to identify a subset of this section to produce a small demonstration system.

ICL, who supplied the mainframe, were selected as the main contractors for the project.

A phased approach to the project was adopted, with separate funding for each phase, the funding for one phase being dependent on the success of the previous one.

8.3.2 The project

The project was split into 4 phases. In phase 1 a feasibility study was conducted to determine whether an expert system could (potentially) be developed to aid in the administration of the TSS. This phase also identified a suitable subset of the TSS which could be used to explore the expert system in depth.

This initial stage required a large commitment from the DES's expert. It is claimed that a man-week of effort from the consultant knowledge engineer and 3 man-weeks effort from the in-house expert were necessary.

This illustrates an important point. There will be a need, even in the earliest stages of the development of an expert system, to gain access to the expert. The expert's time can be almost as fully occupied as the knowledge engineer's, and even more so at some stages. One of the problems with expert systems is that they are normally built whilst the expert is engaged in the day to day exercise of his knowledge. This can lead to problems when unreasonable demands are made on the expert. This is even more of a problem in the not uncommon case where the expert system is being built to relieve pressure on the expert who was 100% committed at the start of the development. If this is the case there needs to be a high level of commitment from senior management and an appreciation that short-term losses will rapidly become gains once the system is completed. In this case this commitment was present, as was an external source of help and advice (in the form of the Treasury's Central Computer and Telecommunications Agency).

Once the suitable subset had been identified ICL recommended the use of the SAGE expert system shell to develop a small expert system, which would represent a subset of the subset.

The DES made no commitment to the purchase of either software or hardware at this point.

The demonstration system built in phase 2 was intended to provide a working example of an expert system. This allows the users and the managers to more fully understand the concepts of the expert system. It explores the feasibility in a relatively cheap way and it tests the viability of the hardware, software and the knowledge engineering.

The most important output from the phase was a working expert system. Until this point the DES had little knowledge about expert systems and the problem being tackled.

Again, the effort required to build this system was split between the knowledge engineer and the expert (4 man-weeks knowledge engineer, 2 man-weeks DES expert).

Phase 3 of the project was aimed at producing a pilot system which incorporated a larger part of the TSS rules, and also served to illustrate further the application of expert systems to the problem.

Another important aspect of the project was illustrated during this phase. The DES intended to maintain and extend the system using in-house expertise developed over the course of the project, so software was developed on a PERQ which allowed DES staff to construct and maintain appropriate SAGE models.

The effort was split almost 50/50 between knowledge engineer (15 man-weeks) and expert (12 man-weeks).

At the end of phase 3 a demonstration system had been built which was deemed satisfactory by both the DES and the CCTA.

Phase 4 of the project consolidated the work done so far and converted it for use on the ICL mainframe (from SAGE to ADVISER).   Additionally, phase 4 aimed to provide an interface between the expert system and the teachers' database.

It is in this phase of the project that the development was substantially different from other expert system projects. Not only was the software conversion necessary but also a special purpose COBOL program was required so that the system could successfully interface with the existing system (see fig 8.5).

This was a success but obviously the need to use the existing system must constrain what it is possible for the expert system to achieve.

At the end of phase 4 the system was successfully demonstrated and the development and maintenance was left with the user (the Pensions Branch).

A phased approach proved very successful at tackling a sub-set of a large and complex problem. The expert system was able to integrate with an existing facility and seemingly provide a value added service. As yet no formal evaluation of usage and benefit accrued by the use of the system has been reported, but the DES appears to be satisfied that the project has been a success.

The problem with the DES expert system was the need to integrate it into existing systems. This had implications for the design of the interface and the constraints which it put on the design.

The system had to remain live throughout the process and the development of the stand-alone small system on advanced equipment enabled a prototyping approach to be adopted without interfering with the main system.

The key interface issues in the design of the system were:

- the user population was already defined and the users had specific experience of using the computer system without the inclusion of an expert system element

- the system was highly constrained by the need to interface with the existing system, which for example,

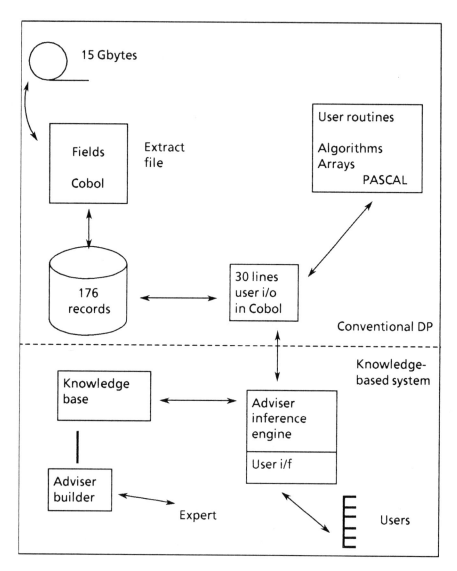

Fig 8.5   Overall architecture of DES expert system

prevented the system builders from using such novel
interface tools as WIMP systems

● the knowledge of the users should be exploited in such a
way that they could provide many of the design
solutions, and thus gain a 'stake' in the final solution.

The second point in a commonly occurring problem in the development of expert systems. It is rarely economic to introduce new hardware to operate an expert system, and even when this is possible, the difficulties of interfacing to the existing hardware often render this infeasible.

This often limits the power of the expert system. The full complexity of many types of knowledge cannot be successfully communicated through the narrow bandwidth imposed by traditional mainframe terminals, for example.

The third issue identified above is one of the key features of good human factors design in all arenas, not just the knowledge-based systems world. The DES system provides an excellent example of the benefits to be reaped from the use of a participative approach to design.

8.4 UCW EXPERT - AN EXAMPLE OF THE PRACTICAL APPLICATION OF SMALL-SCALE EXPERT SYSTEM TOOLS

The RAF supply control centre (RAFSCC) is based at Hendon. However, it has many subsidiaries and these are distributed throughout the UK and West Germany. Each subsidiary has a mini-computer with on-line communications links to the main, Hendon-based, system. Although some expertise resides at each unit, the main repository of knowledge regarding the common faults with the computer is an expert support group on the Hendon site. This support group is known as the UCW.

During 1985, it became apparent that staff losses would shortly have a major impact on the size of the support group. In particular, there was concern that the UCW would be unable to carrry out a major function - acting as a telephone help line for the individual units. A decision was taken that computer based assistance would be required to aid the relatively inexperienced staff who would be called upon to deal with these requests and carry out the telephone based fault diagnosis.

After some initial evaluation, an expert system approach was chosen as the most likely to meet all the requirements. Three principal benefits were seen as arising from the chosen approach:

- an expert system would contain a store of expert knowledge available to less expert staff in fault diagnosis

- an expert system would act as a training aid

- an expert system would increase the efficiency of the unit and possibly reduce the need for new staff as the size of the distributed system increases.

A PC-based shell was selected as the vehicle for the development. This shell was selected largely on the grounds of economy. As expert systems are relatively unproven technology, there was concern about the size of the investment and the speculative nature of the project.

The Xi shell was used. At the time the project was initiated this product had a fuller range of features than its similarly priced competitors. Xi is described from a user's standpoint in Chapter 9. However, we will summarise the main features of the product:

- The knowledge representation is in the form of if-then rules and facts

- Keywords 'is-a' and 'of' at first appear to supply the rudiments of a frame-based system, but the absence of any support renders these of little value

- Various combinations of forward and backward chaining search strategies may be employed

- The system allows the use of 'demons' where a demon comprises:

  when <condition> then <control command>. This can be used to impose some control of the chaining process

- Xi allows the linking of knowledge bases

- Xi automatically constructs multi-choice menus where appropriate

- Xi is able to generate explanations (simple rule traces are provided) and has a built in 'what-if' function.

The task which the expert system was to aid in was the diagnosis of faults in local minicomputers. It is common for the relatively unknowledgable users at individual sites to encounter faults which they are unable to resolve. To support these users, the RAF operates a central advice bureau. Remote sites are able to telephone this centre and ask questions about their problems. Unfortunately, the experts who are able to deal with these queries are not always available, and the system is intended to enable relatively inexperience personnel to deal with these queries. In addition, it was intended that the system would serve as an archive of knowledge which would enable rare expertise to be captured before experts moved on to new postings away from the stores system.

The user population would typically be RAF personnel, possessing a limited degree of familiarity with both the the Honeywell systems and with the PC running the expert system.

Constraints were imposed on the design of the system by employing the expert system shell. The equipment capable of running the shell was a PC or equivalent. The interface characteristics have been largely defined by the company selling the shell and the designer must work within these limitations.

The RAF's expert system consists of seven linked knowledge bases describing the problem. These are:

- Entry

- Startup problems

- Closedown problems

- Hardware faults

- Software faults

- Fault logging

- Useful information.

The entry knowledge base is the first point of access to the system. It contains site-specific information such as configuration details for each site. Thus once the caller's site has been identified, no further questions relating to equipment are required. This implies that the system must be kept up-to-date and might impose a significant maintenance problem depending on how often the site details change. Fortunately, Xi provides a relatively easy replacement/alteration mechanism to the knowledge base, so provided the system has been well-written, alteration of that type of information should be easily achievable.

In a typical telephone query, the first stage is to define the site from which the query originates. The general area of the system at fault (eg hardware, software) is then identified.

Once this basic information has been obtained, the system then enters a question and answer session using one of four knowledge bases described below. The person using the system is more or less constrained to answer questions in the set order prescribed by the system. As each question is answered, a new screen appears, until eventually a proposed solution is arrived at. Thus the interaction is highly constrained and the originator of the query must follow a rigid order which is determined by the system, with fairly poor control over the direction of the session.

The next four knowledge bases (startup, closedown, hardware and software) deal with the actual process of diagnosing the faults. The divisions are clearly arbitrary and are included essentially to ensure that each knowledge base remains a managable size. There are disadvantages to this. If, for example, a standard software problems occurs at an early stage of system startup an inexperienced operator might waste time investigating startup problems.

The sixth knowledge base (fault logging) is essentially a procedural attachment. It is invoked when an apparently genuine bug is encountered and automatically generates a form for logging faults with Honeywell, the computer equipment manufacturer.

The seventh knowledge base, 'Useful Information,' is a largely separate entity. It is little more than a text retrieval system which provides a quantity of useful information relating to a particular subject.

Overall the system contains over 300 rules.   Whilst this might, at first sight, appear a fairly small number of rules, the system is not yet complete. It is able to deal adequately with hardware problems, and with some software faults. Although it is not yet applicable to all software problems, it nevertheless meets a real need and is genuinely used by the users.

The system is currently in daily use, and any criticisms must recognise that this is a very unusual situation. As yet, few expert systems are used 'in anger'. To some extent the problems with interfacing are not very important. The system is essentially quite simple. The task is unvarying from one session to the next. The users have, generally, a very high level of previous exposure to computers, and use the system on a regular basis.

There do appear to be three areas in which improvement could be made. It is worth considering these in detail because each is a reflection of the problems associated with expert system shells and contains a number of general lessons.

The first problem relates to a question which we have already touched upon, that of linked knowledge bases. The system builders themselves have noted an undesirable consequence of this: the performance of Xi tails off when linked knowledge bases are in use. Furthermore, the use of linked knowledge bases can cause difficulties in supplying explanations of chains of reasoning. If the rules that initiated a chain of reasoning form part of a module no longer resident in memory they cannot be presented as part of an explanation. Equally, the power of the 'what-if' function is limited, for similar reasons.

This raises the issue of whether using modules in the first place was a good idea. The reason that modules are used is to provide structure. In Xi (and other rule-based shells) modularisation is the only way to impose structure. The problems described above all arise because one large knowledge base has been split into seven. This is not ideal; a far better solution would be to structure a knowledge base into sections whilst maintainig it as one entity. However, when modifying a particular rule in an Xi knowledge base, the only unique way to refer to it is as 'rule number 5' or even 'rule number 300'!

This contrasts with the graphical displays described in the ESCORT case study.

In fact, the effect of modularisation on explanation quality has not been fully felt by the RAF system developers. This is because of a second problem encountered. The use of a simple 'if-then' rule format constrains the complexity of the control structure possible and makes it difficult to represent procedural knowledge. The answering of a telephone query at Hendon is actually a fairly well defined process and is shown in figure 8.6.

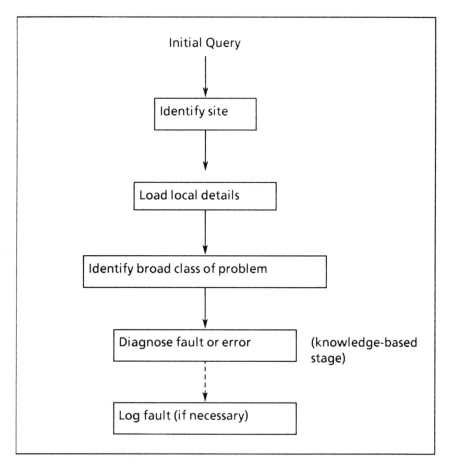

Fig 8.6   UCW Telephone queries

It is important to note, from fig 8.6, that the only stage at which knowledge-based techniques are really needed is the identification stage - one of the six. Rule based systems were originally designed to perform this identification or classification exercise e.g. Mycin, the first, was used to identify blood diseases. Thus it is difficult for the other stages of UCW Expert to take advantage of a rule-based approach. These phases are essentially procedural. One effect of this is to render the explanation system a liability except for the developers. Another, more important effect, is the presence of rules in the knowledge-base which are obscure and difficult to understand . These rules form part of a procedure, rather than being declarative statements, and therefore can not be read in isolation from the rules with which they interact.

The problem is recurrent. Many of the 'simple' problems for which micro-based shells are currently being used have similar characteristics; ie a problem which is only part knowledge-based, the rest being procedural.

Another example is a system designed by one of the authors to help users fill in a complex form. Only two fields were difficult to complete, and the rest of the form required a simple procedural approach. This system was eventually written in Prolog, a language which has both procedural and declarative characteristics, making it the most natural choice for the problem, though requiring a greater level of skill and experience in the system builder.

The main lesson which can be drawn from the use of the smaller shells is that a task with a significant procedural content should use the shell only in certain areas. Alternatively, be prepared to use a distorted representation of the procedure. Ideally the aim should be to combine the two types of knowledge - procedural and declarative. As most shells provide an interface to external programming languages, it might be possible to design a system which invokes the rule-based parts as and when required. Ideally, the link should be reversed, but very few shells can be invoked from external programs as yet.

Another problem with shells is that much of the information contained in the system is better expressed graphically. Thus in the UCW example information relating to communications and to datapaths would be far easier to express in graphical form. The development of lower cost workstations incorporating high resolution graphics displays will lead to the development of a far richer range of tools and facilities which will remove some of these problems.

The main disadvantages with small, shell-based systems seem to be:

- Lack of internal knowledge-base structure

- Poor facilities for handling procedural tasks

- Lack of graphics capabilities.

The main advantages are:

- A system can be built which works

- The system can be constructed quickly without specialised knowledge engineering experts

- The non-procedural aspects are easily modifiable.

8.5 CONCLUSIONS

In general, small shells serve to illustrate the advantages of expert systems. In the DES example, a shell convinced the DES of the advantages of continuing the project. They do, however, have human factors problems. The interface can be idiosyncratic but they can also be used to clearly show the advantages of an expert systems aproach.

In terms of the interfacing issues associated with the development of expert systems, it is important to realise the constrains imposed on developments. Shells have interfaces which are defined by the suppliers and might not necessarily be appropriate to the specific application. Similarly, the need to integrate expert systems with existing systems imposes severe limitations on designers.

The most successful applications of expert systems consider the user and the design of the interface at the very beginning of the development process. The range of options available should not be constrained by the technology, as has all too often been the case in the past

In this chapter we have seen different approaches to the construction of expert systems. In the case of ESCORT, the use of powerful interface tools has enabled the development of a powerful interface. Interestingly, the most complex interface is that to the knowledge.

In two other systems, we have seen simple problems addressed by less powerful tools, and investigated some of the difficulties that shells, for example, can cause.

The choice of tool is clearly of importance. In the next chapter, we investigate the available options.

8.6 REFERENCES

1. Hanes LF, O'Brien JF & DiSalvo R, (1982) 'Control room design: lessons from TMI', IEEE Spectrum, June 1982

2. Fitts P M, 'Functions of men in complex systems,' Aerospace Engineering, 21, 1, pp 34-39 (an update of this work can be found in ' Human Factors of IT in the Office,' B Christie, Wile & Sons, 1985)

3. New Scientist, 18 Aug 1977

4. Sargeant RAES, (1986) 'Expert systems for process control', Measurement and Control Vol 19

5. Sachs, Paterson & Turner, (1986) 'ESCORT - an expert system for conplex operations in real time', Expert Systems, Vol 3, No 1

6. Paterson & Sachs, (1986) 'Causal Reasoning in a real-time expert system', Proc Expert systems and AI in Industry

9

Commercially available tools

9.1 INTRODUCTION

This chapter will address the question of the commercial tools available for expert systems and HCI developments. The main focus is on expert systems, where a plethora of tools are currently available. By contrast, very few tools are aimed explicitly at interface development, but those that exist are described.

The analysis of expert system tools is heavily focused on their interface building qualities: readers interested in other aspects, such as knowledge representation formalisms, inference techniques, etc., should look elsewhere (eg (1)). However, brief descriptions have been found necessary as a basis for understanding the interface tools.

9.2 EXPERT SYSTEM DEVELOPMENT TOOLS - AN OVERVIEW

The tools available for expert system developments break down into three major areas: shells, languages and toolkits. Inevitably there are some tools which do not fit neatly into any of these categories, either because they fall entirely outside them (an example are tools for carrying out rule induction, as described in Chapter 7) or because they span the boundaries. However, the distinctions are still useful in constructing a taxonomy of tools.

9.2.1 Shells

Expert system shells are essentially expert systems with the knowledge removed. Thus one is left with an inference engine, some structures for storing knowledge, and a few other features such as an explanation mechanism. Most shells offer a limited knowledge representation (generally rule-based), fairly low purchase prices, and are generally microcomputer-based. The inferencing techniques on offer will normally be backward and forward chaining, or possibly some mixture of the two. Most of the current crop allow the system builder to impose some metalevel control on the shell, or in other words, to interrupt and redirect the inferencing. This is typically done by writing 'demons', which are statements of the general form 'when (some condition) then perform (some control action - such as switching the rule-chaining, or perhaps scheduling a new goal)'.

Whether microcomputer or mainframe based, the interfaces provided by shells are fairly limiting. The use of a simple chaining inference mechanism means that most applications developed using rule-based shells are characterised by a question-and-answer dialogue, which is virtually wholly machine-driven. A further problem is that the relatively limited screen resolution of mainframe and PC terminals limits the interaction to concepts which can be verbally expressed. One or two suppliers have started to address these problems, by, for example, providing hooks into popular graphics packages, but the level of integration leaves much to be desired. Other approaches which have been used include, for example, the attachment of a video system to display images alongside the shell.

As with most other microcomputer packages, shells often allow the use of windows to improve the quality of the interaction; for example, the answer to a 'why' question can be placed in a pop-up menu, which will not disturb the main flow of the consultation.

The style of interaction (machine-driven) is not, perhaps, as big a problem as it might seem at first sight. Although we have stressed throughout this book the importance of a mixed initiative style of dialogue, this only comes into its own when the tasks being addressed are either numerous or complicated. In fact, most of the expert systems that are constructed using shells tend to be simple systems, designed to answer only one of a few potential queries, each of which follows much the same path.

The other problems we have noted relate to the lack of display facilities. These are certainly a problem for the system user, but have more far-reaching consequences for the system builder. The majority of shells do not allow the grouping or structuring of rules within an application in anything but very crude ways. Couple this with the lack of graphical displays, and the builder of a system with more than perhaps 50-100 rules must either memorise all the identifiers in use, or spend long periods searching through a knowledge base for specific items. The arrival of more powerful tools, perhaps frame-based, on microcomputers, has exacerbated the problem - it is very difficult to understand an inheritance hierarchy of any size without a graphical representation. Indeed, such tools are probably only suitable for the delivery on a PC of systems developed on more powerful hardware until better graphical displays appear on PCs.

Similar problems arise in debugging knowledge bases - a graphical display of a chain of reasoning is far easier to understand than a written one.

The third major area of consideration for interface specialists is the interface to the knowledge base. Ideally, a system builder will construct an interface to the knowledge base which will enable the expert and the user associated with the system to modify that knowledge base without the intervention of the system builder. This interface will therefore present the system's knowledge in ways which are natural to people working in the domain, rather than to expert system specialists. Also, the interface may protect, for example, the code which controls the process of carrying out the task, and only allow the modification of that knowledge which is applied to that task.

Very few shells allow the development of such interfaces. In the main, there is one interface for system modification, which is used by all parties. Perhaps the main drawback with this interface is that anyone intending to modify the knowledge base must understand the system in some detail. Most such systems employ interfaces which are quite difficult to relearn, and this can cause problems where (as is quite common, particularly in simple systems) the knowledge only requires to be amended infrequently.

Having made a number of criticisms of shells, it is only fair to reflect on the benefits they offer. Most provide a very inexpensive tool, that enables even quite inexperienced personnel to both learn about expert systems, and to construct simple systems very quickly. As we have discussed, some of the limits on the interaction are imposed by the simplicity of the systems typically built using shells, and others by the simple nature of the reasoning employed by the shells.

Section 9.5.1 describes the highlights of some of the many commercially available shells. Particularly in the UK, the expert system tool market is dominated (at least in terms of quantity) by shells, and the list presented is therefore only representative.

9.2.2 Languages

Expert systems can be constructed in any computer language. However, most computer languages are designed to be suited to certain styles of programming, and to certain types of application. Two computer languages are generally regarded as being suited to the development of expert systems; these are Prolog and Lisp.

Prolog has long been the favoured tool of a large segment of the European AI community. Prolog (PROgramming in LOGic) grew out of research work in the areas of logic and theorem proving carried out at the University of Marseilles. As a development tool, its strengths are:

- a good formal structure. Prolog is an implementation of first order predicate calculus, and although the purity of the implementation has been sullied by the need to provide, for example, input-output facilities, it still makes programs capable of analysis

- a dual nature. Most Prolog programs can be read in two ways. Firstly, procedurally, as with most programming languages. Secondly, declaratively, as with if-then rules. This dual nature makes Prolog partly suited to both representing knowledge as a collection of items or clauses (declarative reading) and the program which accesses that knowledge (procedure). The extent to which any programming language can satisfy two such disparate goals is a moot point; Prolog is necessarily a compromise, and as such is not a good choice unless both readings are genuinely useful.

- a powerful approach to constructing arbitrary structures. Thus it is possible to fairly easily define complex structures which can represent knowledge naturally

- a built-in inference engine. The first order predicate calculus enables the construction of a backward chaining system with the greatest of ease.

Unfortunately, Prolog does not lend itself easily to the development of interactive systems. As mentioned earlier, from the standpoint of Prolog as an implementation of logic, input and output is an illogical side effect. Perhaps because of its academic genesis, Prolog has long lacked the facilities to ease the construction of good interfaces. Some new arrivals on the scene have started to address these problems, but there is more to be done to achieve the standards set by some Lisp versions (see below). A further recent advance has been the development of incremental compilers for Prolog, which are an invaluable aid in the development process.

Alternatively, Prolog can be viewed as just one tool to be employed in the building of a system, rather than as the vehicle for the whole system. This approach was discussed for rule-based shells during Chapter 8, but the same comments apply to Prolog (if anything, they are more valid for Prolog, because Prolog offers more flexibility for addressing unusual problems, and is therefore likely to be used in systems which do require other specialised tools). This approach has not been widely adopted - exceptions are the Knowledge Craft toolkit (see section 9.5.3) and POPLOG.

Lisp (LISt Processing) has a lengthy pedigree. It is (behind Fortran) the second oldest computer programming language still in widespread use. The language has two distinguishing features when compared to other languages, and it is these which have endeared it to the AI world:

- the language is functionally oriented. This makes it easy to produce highly modularised code, and makes it possible to provide for Lisp a programming support environment which goes beyond those available for other languages. It also makes Lisp an ideal vehicle for implementing an object-oriented development system

- the language is designed for processing symbols rather than numbers.

Lisp has been heavily used by research groups in the USA. Over time, other activities of researchers in such groups have led to Lisp possessing two massive advantages as a basis for IKBS development work, so important that it becomes necessary to distinguish between Lisp and 'Lisp plus'. Straightforward implementations of Lisp are comparable to Prolog for the quality of their input-output facilities.

The first factor has been the development of computers with specialised hardware architectures, designed explicitly to run Lisp programs very fast. These machines are typically expensive single user workstations, and are usually provided with large bit-mapped high resolution displays, and a mouse.

The second factor is the development environments supplied with such machines. The first developments of WIMP systems took place at much the same place and time as early AI research, and not surprisingly, the ideas were taken up with great enthusiasm. The net result is that the programmer gains through the availability of high level tools for the construction of window-based interfaces which allow for much graphics, and interaction via a mouse rather than keyboard. This means that the development of systems can iterate around the design-build loop much faster, enabling the trying out of more different approaches in the prototyping stages of system development. This rapid prototyping approach to interface construction allows the eventual user more say in the shaping of the interface, increasing the likelihood of the system's final acceptance.

The quality of interface is extended to the programmer, who will be provided with high quality editors, graphical displays of procedure calling, and so on.

Thus Lisp used on a Lisp machine has a number of advantages, the most important of which are the quality of the development environment, the ability to rapidly prototype, and the power to run Lisp at high speed.

The disadvantages are twofold: cost and human resources. Such systems cost upwards of £20000 for a single user workstation. Furthermore, they require skilled users to extract the maximum benefit, and there is currently a shortage of such skills. Section 9.5.2 describes some of the commonly available Lisp machines and their associated software environments. Versions of Lisp are available which do not incorporate powerful development environments, and do not require specialist hardware; such are not listed, largely because there is little to choose between the alternatives from the point of view of the interface constructor.

9.2.3 Toolkits

Whilst the languages described above are well suited to the development of expert systems, neither provides built-in structures for representing knowledge in a variety of ways.

As we noted earlier, shells solve these problems by providing a predetermined knowledge representation structure, and a built-in inference engine. There are dangers with this - principally that the particular representation and inferencing may not be appropriate to the applicationat hand, and worse, that this may not be immediately apparent.

As will emerge in Chapter 10, our favoured approach to the development of complex expert systems is an iterative cycle, with frequent referral to the expert. One of the reasons underlying these recommendations is that knowledge engineering is a very young science. A large number of expert system development projects involve tackling completely novel problems, and in this situation the most appropriate structure for the knowledge bases will not be immediately apparent. Using a shell may prematurely impose a structure (usually that of if-then rules) on a problem to which another approach is better suited. Even at the best this is likely to mean that the knowledge base is not natural, and therefore difficult for the expert to update. Also, the user-system dialogue may be unduly lengthy, with the system unable to provide explanations in terms the user can understand. At the worst, a poor choice of knowledge representation may render the expert system incapable of answering certain types of query.

The solution to these problems is the use of a 'toolkit ' in the critical early stages of development. Toolkits are characterised by a wide range of options for knowledge representation and inferencing. These options will typically include:

- if-then rules - either with chaining or some other produciton rule system

- object-oriented programming, coupled with a frame-based hierarchy. See for example the plant representation in the Escort case study. The attractions of this approach are enhanced when coupled with graphic display tools

- access-oriented programming - where reading or writing some data value causes a function to be called

- uncertainty - some statistical techniques for handling uncertainty may be available

- truth maintenance - where the system keeps track of the the premises which underly each item currently believed to be true

- worlds - an extension of truth maintenance, where the truth maintenance information is used to maintain a number of different 'worlds', differentiated by the set of assumptions on which each is founded, and hence containing different sets of derived hypotheses.

Thus toolkits are characterised by a richness of representation. This is combined with good graphics tools - providing both systen builder and user with a comfortable environment. Until recently, these toolkits have only been available on AI workstations, and have been founded on the powerful Lisp environments described earlier. Recently, other versions have appeared, written in for example 'C'. These have been ported to more conventional hardware, but still generally to powerful single user Unix workstations, thus maintaining the link with WIMPs (windows, icons, mice and pointing interfaces), high resolution graphics and powerful single user computing. All these help in the task at which toolkits excel - supporting a tight cycle of iteration in the prototyping phase.

There are enormous advantages to be gained from the speed at which prototyping can therefore be carried out. Two particular areas are firstly situations where the ultimate functions of the system are poorly defined, and secondly those where there is not a relevant precedent for the system. The first case is a recurrent problem in the development of expert systems at the time of writing; many potential users have been made aware that 'AI is going to change the way they do business,' but their lack of understanding of AI techniques (coupled with the lack of understanding of their problems on the part of the AI specialists) prevents the requirements on the system from being clearly specified at the outset. Rather, a dialogue develops, as the AI developer suggests some functionality, the user suggests something else by analogy, the developer points up a few limitations, the user tries something else, and so on.

Alternatively, even when the requirement is clear, the means of satisfying it may not be. This is inevitable in the use of a new technology such as IKBS. The best solution is to try as many approaches as possible; the toolkit makes this possible in an acceptable time frame.

Table 9.5.3 describes the most popular toolkits.

9.3 SUMMARY

Table 9.1 summarises the pros and cons of the different classes of IKBS tool we have identified.

We have tried to make a strong case for the use of toolkits in the prototyping phase. Indeed, it is our opinion that for the development of any reasonably complex (say a total of more

	Pros	Cons

Shells	Easy to use - simple
	
	Cheap
	
	Good for :-
	  - training
	  - small diagnostic
	    tasks
	  - regulations
		Inflexible knowledge representation
		
		Poor for prototyping
		
		Mediocre HCI

Languages	Highly flexible
	
	Good for:
	  - natural language
	  - very unusual tasks
	  - fast performance
		Difficult to use
		
		Slow to produce results

Toolkits	Very powerful
	
	Good for:
	  - prototyping
	  - difficult HCI
	  - tasks requiring a
	    range of
	    techniques
		Very expensive
		
		Quite difficult to use

Table 9.1   Pros and Cons of different classes of IKBS
development tool

than 1 man year of effort) system, this will inevitably be the
most efficient approach.

However, this does not in any way mean that the delivery
vehicle should be a Lisp machine complete with toolkit. In
many cases it may be found, that at the end of the prototyping
phase, the subset of techniques available in the toolkit that are
in use for a particular application are available within either a
shell, or perhaps one of the PC-based object systems (see
section 9.5.3). Referring to the methodology advocated in
Chapter 10, it is likely that at the end of the prototyping

phase, all the technical problems will have been overcome, but
only a small subset of the full system will have been
implemented. Thus the costs of transferring at this stage are
likely to be relatively low. Fig 9.1 shows a possible role for

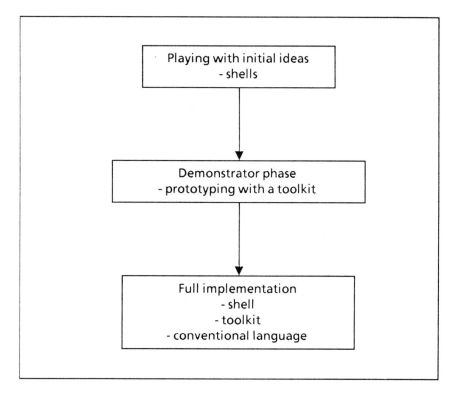

Fig 9.1   IKBS tools in thedevelopment cycle

different tools to play in the development of a large scale
expert system.

9.4 CONCLUSIONS

AI is a rapidly changing field. Our view of the commercially
available tools is based on data gathered in 1986/7. We do not
expect the scene to remain static. However, the main aim of
the chapter has been to present a snapshot of the field and to
discuss the broad issues governing classes of development
tools.

In the next chapter we will examine a methodology which will incorporate the ideas developed in the preceding chapters. It will emphasise the importance of some of the factors which we have tried to draw out in this chapter.

9.5 THE TOOLS

This section is not intended to be exhaustive. Rather, it provides a hopefully representative sample of what is a vailable in the three main classes of tool we have described.

Most of the descriptions are based on first hand experience of use in anger: otherwise, company literature and demonstrations have served as a substitute source of information.

9.5.1 Shells

9.5.1.1 Xi Plus

SUPPLIER: Expertech Ltd
                 Expertech House
                 172 Bath Rd
                 Slough
                 Berks SL1 3XE

COST: £1200

HARDWARE: IBM PC or compatible

SYSTEM INTERFACE AND KNOWLEDGE REPRESENTATION

Knowledge representation is based on if-then rules, and much attention is paid to achieving an English-like rule syntax. The danger with this otherwise laudable aim is that people updating knowledge might not realise the need to understand the syntax. Procedural knowledge is entered using demons, which can lead to the 'knowledge base' containing some rather obscure looking constructs.
Modification of the knowledge base is via a poor screen editor. There is no possibility of constructing a separate interface to the knowledge base for user use.
A dictionary of identifiers is available to ease access to a large knowledge base.

The only way to partition sections of the knowledge base is through linking separate knowledge bases at run time.

USER INTERFACE

Multi-choice menus are constructed automatically where appropriate. A built-in 'why' facility will regurgitate the rules used in the current chain of reasoning. Canned explanatory text may be associated with questions. A 'what-if' facility is also included, but the use of forward chaining rules (demons) to control the procedure the system follows can make this a confusing business.
In general, the interface must be used as supplied, rather than redefined to suit the system builder.

9.5.1.2 Crystal

SUPPLIER: Intelligent Environments
               20 Crown Passage
               St James's
               London   SW1Y 6PP

COST: £695 (plus external interface options)

HARDWARE: IBM PC or compatible

SYSTEM INTERFACE AND KNOWLEDGE REPRESENTATION

Similar to Xi Plus. The product runs very fast, and benefits from this. It possesses a reasonable screen editor.
It is rather more difficult to control inferencing than with the Xi Plus shell.
Procedural tasks and sub-tasks are much better represented in Crystal – it allows the system builder to schedule explicitly tasks such as filling in forms.

USER INTERFACE
The interface is flexible. The system builder has the ability to use good quality graphics and pop-up menus to help build a useful interface for the user.
Explanation is the usual rule trace.
Crystal does not have a 'what-if' facility.

9.5.1.3 Personal Consultant Plus

SUPPLIER: Texas Instruments
                 Manton Lane
                 Bedford
                 MK41 7PA

COST :   c. £2000

HARDWARE: IBM PC or compatible, and TI PCs

SYSTEM INTERFACE AND KNOWLEDGE REPRESENTATION

Based on the original Personal Consultant, which was very
Mycin-like in all respects: it supports backward and forward
chaining, and certainty factors for numerically handling
uncertainty.
The system is Lisp-based which may be an advantage for those
delivering systems prototyped in Lisp.
The 'Plus' version of the system includes two interesting
features: a rudimentary frame-based system, and the ability to
build high level controls for rule application. Thus one can
escape the limitations of pure chaining when tackling slightly
unusual problems.
The interface to the knowledge is by forms, and appears
effective.

USER INTERFACE

A window and menu-based system - the system builder has
little control over the style of interface presented to the user.

9.5.1.4 Savoir

SUPPLIER: ISI
                 11 Oakdene Rd
                 Redhill
                 Surrey RH1 6BT

COST :   Price varies from £3000-£15000 dependent
                 upon hardware

HARDWARE: Various PCs, Sage minis, Vax's, IBM
                 mainframes

SYSTEM INTERFACE AND KNOWLEDGE REPRESENTATION

The system is written in Pascal, and has been ported to an impressive array of machines, which may prove attractive for large organisations.
The representation of if-then rules is slightly unusual, and encourages the user to regard the rulebase as a network.
The system suffers from the fact that knowledge bases must be compiled, thus slowing down the time to iterate around the prototyping loop.
Savoir has a useful and fairly well thought-out demon system for control of reasoning.

USER INTERFACE

The display is configurable to suit the user, but little use is made of graphics or of window-based interfaces.
A viewdata interface exists to this shell.

9.5.1.5 Envisage/ Adviser

SUPPLIER: (ENVISAGE)   Systems Designers
Pembroke House
Pembroke Broadway
Camberley
Surrey

                (ADVISER)   ICL
Wenlock Way
West Gorton
Manchester M12 5DR

COST :   £2500-£15000 (according to hardware)

HARDWARE: ICL mainframes, Vaxs, IBM PC

SYSTEM INTERFACE AND KNOWLEDGE REPRESENTATION

The system was developed jointly by ICL and SD from the Sage product. ICL market ICL mainframe versions, SD the others.
The system includes a typical if-then trule system. Unusual additions include some concepts borrowed from mainstream computing (eg strong typing, Pascal-style records, interfaces to Pascal and Fortran)

The system uses a concept of 'areas' which enable the knowledge within an application to be parcelled up separately.

USER INTERFACE

The user interface is configurable. For those prepared to invest a large amount of effort, it is worth knowing that the user interface code was developed as a separate module, and could therefore be radically modified.
The system allows multiple windows on a screen, the usual range of explanations, and a 'what-if' facility.
A separate module may be designed by the system builder, to be invoked when the user types help. This seems a genuinely useful idea, as it enables the user, via a help interface to not only get help facilities tailored to the particular application, but perhaps to even change the course of the consultation.

9.5.2 Lisp environments

9.5.2.1 Interlip-D

SUPPLIER: (UK)
                 AIL
                 Intelligence House
                 Merton Rd
                 Watford
                 Herts

COST: Free (with Xerox workstations)

HARDWARE: Xerox 1186 work-stations

SYSTEM INTERFACE AND KNOWLEDGE REPRESENTATION

Full implementation of Lisp. The latest version of the environment supports both Interlisp-D and Common Lisp, but there are doubts about the ability of this environment to support the additional bulk of a toolkit.
As well as Lisp, Interlisp offers a record package (akin to Pascal records), extensions to Lisp to enable For... loops and variants, a well integrated windowing system, and many other extensions to lisp. In addition, the system comes with a large number of packages, each of which implements a more or less general version of some useful facility.

Finally, Interlisp possesses one of the finest interactive development environments, making debugging programs very simple. The mouse driven editor, designed specifically for Lisp programmers, is also very powerful.

USER INTERFACE

Interlisp-D includes a windowing system which uses high level commands and is well integrated with the Lisp. A number of the packages mentioned are useful to the programmer rapidly prototyping variations in the user interface (eg making rectangular regions of a window sensitive to mouse activity). In general, the interfacing software consists of a very wide range of disparate but simple and useful functions, rather than a well engineered whole. The effect of this is that the system is ideally suited for fast prototyping, rather than for well-structured and easily maintainable software developments.

9.5.2.2 Genera-7

SUPPLIER: Symbolics
St Johns Court
Easton St
High Wycombe
Bucks
HP11 1JX(UK)

COST: Free (with Symbolics workstations)

HARDWARE: Symbolics work-station

SYSTEM INTERFACE AND KNOWLEDGE REPRESENTATION

Similar in scope to Interlisp-D. The system does not allow for such powerful interactive development, and the editor (ZMACS), whilst very good by conventional standards, does not measure up to the standard set by the Interlisp system.
Symbolics Lisp does, however possess a major advantage, in that the environment is based on the Flavours object environment. Thus all entities (eg i/o streams, windows, menus, etc) are objects and can thus be manipulated in powerful ways.
In addition, the software benefits from greater uniformity.

USER INTERFACE

Similar to the Interlisp environment, although does not have the same richness of readily available packages that characterises Interlisp. However, these facilities can be rapidly replicated, and the Symbolics does benefit from a cleaner overall structure.
It should be noted that the latest release of Symbolics software (Genera 7) incorporates some extensions to the basic Zetalisp environment which may be of interest to the interface designer. These include particularly the presentation system, a powerful basis for the construction of user interfaces, which has no parallel elsewhere in the industry.

9.5.3 Toolkits

9.5.3.1 KEE

SUPPLIER: Intellicorp
                 Runnymede Malthouse
                 Runnymede Rd
                 Egham
                 Surrey
                 TW20 9BO

COST: £30000 (less for further copies)

HARDWARE: Various workstations
                 (NB. KEE is only available under Lisp)

SYSTEM INTERFACE AND KNOWLEDGE REPRESENTATION

The first of the commercial toolkits, with by far the largest installed base worldwide. Supports frames, inheritance, etc, with a good and graphical interactive interface for modifying the parts of the object hierarchy.
KEE incorporates a truth maintenance system and a Worlds system.
The quality of the KEE interface makes the system relatively simple both to learn and to use. The quality of the system interface makes this toolkit particularly suited to rapid prototyping.
KEE's rule system is slow (although a compiler is promised at the time of writing) and the range of control strategy possibilities is relatively limited.

Intellicorp, unlike their competitiors, are not currently investing effort in producing non-Lisp versions of the toolkit.

USER INTERFACE

The system incorporates KEE Pictures, an object-oriented graphics world containing some very useful software. Also interesting is the active images facility, which enables graphical displays to be attached to, and to vary with, the contents of slots.
Also supplied with KEE is Common Windows, a proposed extension to Common Lisp for windows, menus, etc. Because this is supplied with all versions of KEE, it has the potential to make porting KEE applications much easier (most of the work in porting between Lisp versions is in rewriting the interface functions).

9.5.3.2 Art

SUPPLIER: Inference Corp
                (UK distributors
                Ferranti
                Ty Coch Way
                Cwmbran
                Gwent
                NP44 7XX)

COST: £75000 (less for further copies)

HARDWARE: Various workstations
                (NB. KEE is only available under Lisp)

SYSTEM INTERFACE AND KNOWLEDGE REPRESENTATION

Places relatively little emphasis on objects, preferring to concentrate on rules and facts (and thus is perhaps more easily related to a shell). Thus object-oriented porgramming is a relatively new arrival within Art.
Otherwise, Art has the same range of features as KEE, plus numerical techniques for handling uncertainty, and a greater range of control possibilities. It does not have the same quality of interactive development interface.

USER INTERFACE

Has no equivalent of active images, and in general takes more effort to generate portable interfaces.

9.5.3.3 Knowledge Craft

SUPPLIER: Carnegie (UK) Ltd
                 GSI House
                 Stanhope Rd
                 Camberley
                 Surrey   GU15 3PS

COST: £50000 (less for further copies)

HARDWARE: Various workstations

SYSTEM INTERFACE AND KNOWLEDGE REPRESENTATION

Has a very complete and powerful frame and object system.
Rather than defining its own rule system, Knowledge Craft simply incorporates OPS-5 and Prolog (OPS-5 is a forward chaining rule language).
In general, Knowledge Craft has probably slightly more complete functionality than ART or KEE, but the interface does not provide quite the same prototyping speed (especially when compared to KEE's object system)

UER INTERFACE

9.5.3.4 Gold Works

SUPPLIER: Gold Hill Inc
                 (UK distributors :
                 AIL
                 Intelligence House
                 58-78 Merton Rd
                 Watford
                 Herts   WD1 7BY

COST: £5000

HARDWARE: (IBM PCs and compatibles – Gold Hill also supply a plug-in 80386 board for enhanced performance at £7000)

SYSTEM INTERFACE AND KNOWLEDGE REPRESENTATION

Has a frame-based system but with one or two limitations. Only leaf nodes in the inheritance hierarchy can be treated as objects, and the structure of frame attributes is limited.

USER INTERFACE

Does not have the same level of built-in tools for constructing graphical interfaces as either Art or KEE, and thus it is likely that interfaces will take longer to construct.

9.6 REFERENCES

1. Reichgelt H, Harmelin F Van, (1986) 'Criteria for choosing representation languages and control regiomes for expert system,' Knowledge Engineering Review, Vol 1 No 4

10

A User-Centred Approach to the Design of IKBS

10.1 INTRODUCTION

We have described many different aspects of IKBS and HCI. In this chapter we bring these different parts together and present an HCI-centred approach to the development of large scale expert systems.

In this context 'large scale' is defined as requiring at least 1 man-year of effort to complete. Although we present a complex and rigorous procedure for systems design, smaller projects can employ part of the methodology.

A basic tenet of good IKBS/HCI design is that it should employ the same controls as are applied in conventional systems development. Thus, models of life-cycle systems design and the systems design process models should be applied to expert systems and HCI.

One of the most important points about the methodology is the need to include a phase which allows for some research. This is a reflection of the continuing status of expert systems as predominantly research tools, and the degree to which all new large scale projects are to some extent extending our knowledge of expert systems. This does not imply that expert systems should be considered primarily as research systems. Similarly, the risk involved in the design and construction of expert systems should not necessarily be any greater than in other design processes. Indeed, the aim of developing any design guidelines should be to minimise the risks associated with the construction of expert systems and to ensure that the final system is not only useful but also usable.

We present the approach from a human factors/expert systems viewpoint. This does not mean that traditional DP analysis tools and skills are not required. Many of the crucial parts of the system design require such tools and skills. Our aim is to draw attention to the unique problems and processes associated with expert systems as well as attempting to input human factors in a systematic and useful way.

10.2 OVERVIEW

We have divided the design process into seven phases, based on previously published guidelines on the design of expert systems (7). This is slightly different from other approaches such as Parkin (1) and Shackel (2), but covers the main points raised in these works. We also differ from the HMSO guidelines in that we adopt an integrated human factors/expert systems approach rather than concentrating exclusively on the expert systems aspects.

The 7 phases are:

- Initial study

- Feasibility study

- Prototype development

- System specification

- System implementation

- System evaluation

- System maturation.

These phases will be both human and machine centred. The critical feature of the methodolgy is that it stresses both the human and the system. The human is not only the ultimate end-user but also the expert, the knowledge engineer, the designer and the system support/maintenance operator. Whilst traditional systems have been designed with a minimal degree of user input, expert systems will never be successful without full consideration of the spectrum of the users' needs and requirements. The basic philosophy of expert systems is that they fulfil users' needs in some respect by supplementing their skills.

10.3 DESIGN FOR USABILITY

It is worthwhile outlining five fundamental features of design for usability and considering their applicability to expert systems before detailing the methodology.

10.3.1 User centred design

The design should focus on the users and their tasks from the start. This is especially important in the design of expert systems. It is necessary to focus both on the expert or experts who are supplying the knowledge and on the ultimate end-users of the system. Expert system designers must remember that the advice which the system provides will be required not only by the experts who are supplying the knowledge, but also by end-users who might have little or no knowledge of the problem domain.

10.3.2 Participative design

Whilst we have already pointed out that expert systems must involve experts to supply knowledge, other expected users should work with the design team. The effectiveness of participative design has been documented as long ago as 1948 (3) in the implementation of new procedures into a traditional factory. Subsequent work over the next 40 years has done nothing to dispel the basic message that users are able to provide information which is critical to the success of the system.

The knowledge engineer and system builders should become familiar with the real problems faced by users at an early stage. Knowledge about the problem domain is insufficient in itself. The designer must also know how to convey that knowledge to an expert as well as the expert conveying knowledge to the designer. Consideration of the characteristics and requirements of the end-users prevents a system being designed by experts for use by experts.

10.3.3 Experiment design

Throughout the seven phase process, suitably designed experiments should be carried out to asses the viability of ideas and systems developed during the project. These will investigate not only 'how right' the knowledge is, but also how usable the system is. It is important to employ suitable design and analysis techniques. These should assess aspects of the system in a systematic and unbiased way. It may not be enough to employ ad-hoc questionnaires and informal trials. As expert systems are perceived as being radically different by their users, the role which the system is to play must be explained. Decisions taken on issues such as job security and the system's impact in the work environment must be discussed and explained to those affected. It is a key requirement of the successful introduction of expert systems that some formal experimental design procedure is followed, otherwise the ultimate system may be poorly understood, little used and much resented. Whilst expert systems can and have been successfully designed without these steps being taken, such processes are more risky and the cost of failure may be high. The boundaries of the expert system need to be carefully defined and explained as it is important to define what the system won't do as well as what it will.

10.3.4 Iterative design

All expert systems should ideally be built using an iterative design philosophy. This is explicitly stated many times. However, it is not only the expert who must be consulted and reconsulted, it is also the users. They must be allowed to see their comments employed to produce a better system. They must be shown that the system is designed to be usable and that it will solve their problems.

10.3.5 User/system maintenance

The designer must remember that the user and the system will need supporting and maintaining. The provision of training, help and room for user 'maturation' are essential for successful system design. Of equal importance is the provision of such AI specific features as are genuinely useful, such as explanation, what-ifs, etc. Expert systems provide the opportunity for flexible, usable systems design. The development of the system and the users once the system is complete is an important part of the expert system's success.

10.4 THE APPROACH

10.4.1 Initial study

The initial study should take a few days. The object of the study is to establish some of the salient features of the project. It should detail:

- The need for an expert system to solve the problem.

- Whether the humans who currently meet that need are doing so by the explicit use of expert knowledge in a reasonably constrained area.

- The potential benefits which will be gained by the introduction of an expert system.

- Who the ultimate end-users of the expert system will be.

- Is there a role for an expert system to support a variety of specialists?

The most difficult part of this process is to identify whether the knowledge is reasonably constrained. Expert systems are very poor at carrying out tasks which required a lot of 'common sense'. Tasks which originally appeared amenable to the application of expert systems have failed to meet their original potential. In-depth study of the task has made it clear that the expert system would be required to use not only the expert's knowledge but also a great deal of more general knowledge. It is hard to assess the degree to which general knowledge plays a role. One technique is to work through the task in very small steps, and to assess the degree to which each step employs general knowledge.

It is very important that the likely benefits of the system are assessed at this early stage. These might be in terms of relieving the expert's load so that more time is available for the really difficult problems, or in assessing who and how many end-users would benefit from access to the potential system.

There have been inter-personal problems between experts and end-users in the design of expert systems, and it is important to reassure both groups as to the expert system's abilities and the aim of the project.

In particular, experts should not see the extraction of their expertise and the development of an expert system as an attempt to replace them. It is often a means of supporting them or of relieving them of the more trivial or mundane tasks which they carry out.

Occasionally an expert system might be required to capture expertise which is about to be lost, for example as the result of retirement, resignation or transfer. This requires the designer to build a system which will duplicate the expert's knowledge prior to the expert's departure. It is important that such situations are accurately assessed early on. The expert might be the sole source of information and the end-users will gain substantial benefit from the expert system.

10.4.2 Feasibility study

The objectives of the feasibility study are:

- To produce an overview of the system's capabilities

- To establish that the proposed application is both suited to expert system techniques and that it lies within the bounds of current technology

- To identify more clearly the benefits expected to accrue from the development of the system and to carry out an initial cost-benefit analysis

- To choose a sub-set of the main problem as the basis for a prototype

- To clearly establish the experts and the end-users

- To consider the requirements of the end-user of the expert system

- To lay down the boundaries or limits of the system's scope.

The feasibility study is likely to produce an idea of the capability of the end-system. However, this will not be as clearly defined as a conventional system's feasibility study. It is less easy to concisely describe the operational requirements and potential of the expert system. Users will be less aware of the possibilities and the experts will be less able to understand the system's requirements.

Establishing that the proposed application is techinically feasible requires input from the source of expert knowledge. The expert must be available, probably for one or more concentrated periods lasting about 1 week. Subsequently, the expert should generally be accessible for 1-2 hour sessions over the course of the project. The expert must be a genuine expert, someone who carries out the task regularly, and who is a practitioner rather than a theoretician. As we have already noted, the system must avoid the use of general or common-sense knowledge. It is general knowledge which is the hardest form of knowledge to introduce into an expert system.

The task should involve no more than a few hours of intellectual effort. If it takes more time than this, it is likely to be too complex to automate.

Ideally the expert should be available, enthusiastic and co-operative. The task should be knowledge based in a limited domain. At this stage it is necessary to have the full and whole-hearted co-operation of the expert.

The benefits of the expert system are not always easily measurable in the form of direct cost savings. Some are unique to expert systems, but do provide important gains for both users and experts.

Amongst the benefits which expert systems can provide are:

- The ability to archive scarce knowledge. Consider the example given previously of the expert who is retiring. An expert system provides a method of capturing the lost knowledge in a form which others can employ.

- A method for managing complexity. Some tasks are difficult for humans, not because they are intrinsically difficult, but because they require too many ideas and concepts to be held and employed simultaneously. Whilst humans do deal with complexity fairly well, some problems require too many critical elements to be considered simultaneously. For example, workshop scheduling is a difficult problem purely because there are a large number of constraints and dependent variables to be considered in arriving at any given solution.

- A way of passing skill on. By making the knowledge of an expert available in a form which can be assimilated by others, non-experts are able to operate more skillfully and more efficiently, and gain some of the expert's skills.

- A method of reducing the demand on experts' time. A system which will deal with simple tasks will allow the expert to concentrate on the more complex tasks which are not easily dealt with by an expert system.

- A way of ensuring consistency. Unlike human experts, expert systems do not perform inconsistently under the same circumstances. They do not generally have personal prejudices (though this is another feature of expert systems which are poorly designed and incompletely assessed). An expert system will not have an 'off-day', or a blind spot, etc.

- A training aid. Users will be able to learn, as if consulting with the expert. This is only the case when the interface has been well designed. Often substantial overheads, training, learning to use the system, and on the job training, can all be reduced. A well designed system, with a suitable interface can allow a new user access to an expert who can be used to train and increase the user's skills.

- A tool for recording knowledge which an organisation can use for planning and exploring the implications of strategic plans. Also, the company is provided with a valuable resource, which makes it less dependent on individual experts, more flexible and better able to analyse and exploit its commercial advantage.

- A truly 'user friendly' interface. Despite many claims to the contrary it seems clear that only a system which embodies knowledge about the user will be able to adapt and provide a natural, perhaps individually tailored user interface.

The first four benefits listed have already been achieved (to a greater or lesser extent). As we move down the list the benefits become more speculative and of the nature 'It should be possible...'

The problem with many of these advantages is that they are difficult to quantify. An organisation using expert systems for the first time will probably wish to obtain a quantifiable cost benefit. As experience with the technology grows, the less obvious advantages can be more confidently assessed. They also present a list of criteria against which a completed system can be evaluated.

The feasibility study will also identify a suitable sub-set of the problem for the next phase. This will include a full plan for producing the system to address this sub-set, as well as describing why it was chosen. The sub-set should be sufficiently representative of the overall problem that its successful implementation will enable the designer to accurately assess how to produce the full system, as well as demonstrate the possibilities of the system to others involved.

This is very difficult to achieve. The sub-set should probably be not more than 10% of the overall system. It should be sufficiently independent to demonstrate the advantages of the overall system without requiring excessive simulation.

10.4.3 Prototype construction

This is the key phase in the methodology. As we have already stated, it is important to employ an iterative design process at all stages in the construction of the expert system. Fig 10.1 shows the iterative process for the prototype construction.

The prototype system is the critical stage in the design process because it is the first point at which the benefits of the system can be shown. It is at this stage that special attention has to be paid to the user and to the expert.

An evolutionary systems approach is helpful in the design of an expert system. This is primarily because it is difficult to predict in advance what the most appropriate structures for the knowledge will be. This uncertainty is caused by a number of factors, including the tasks, the expert's knowledge and the user interfaces. It is useful to be able to experiment with different approaches to these problems. The prototype will demonstrate the potential of the system, thus allowing the users to gauge the capabilities of the system.

The process of system design involves the knowledge engineer or designer identifying some of the interesting features of the prototype's domain. This in turn is dependent on input from the expert and from the end-users. Once a limited system can be built the expert can explore its limitations and faults and provide feedback to the designer regarding improvements, alterations, etc. Also, the end-user can explore the system, probably with the expert, and provide comments on ease of use. This should be done in a systematic way.

The suggestions gathered at this stage will often produce a large increase in the system's performance and usability. The important point to remember is that feedback should be shown to be effective - encouraging more expert/user participation. Note, that although we have distinguished between the user and the expert, they need not necessarily be different people, but if the end-users are likely to be markedly different from the expert, they must be actively consulted at this stage.

Throughout this process, the system builders must be prepared to discard developments which for one reason or another do not measure up to the end system's requirements. It is important that the expert and the user are not fettered in the comments which they are allowed to make. It is often

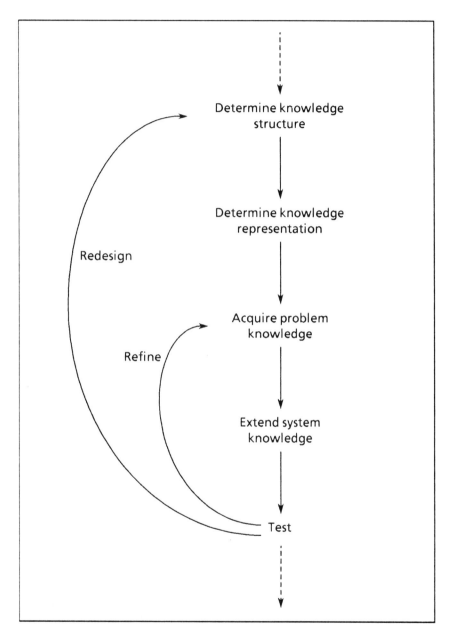

Fig 10.1   Iterative prototyping

difficult to facilitate criticism and to avoid defensive posturing. However, the designer must endeavour to view feedback positively and uncritically, as it might represent the only method of improving the system.

Many of the pyschological techniques for encouraging openness, for promoting lateral thinking, and for providing a different quality of information can be used. For example, formal brainstorming can be instituted to provide information.

Users should not be required to 'bend' their requirements or to adapt their knowledge. Nor should they be required to alter their behaviour to successfully use the system. Mistakes made at this stage will be repeated and magnified in the main system. It may be helpful to give a user representative overall responsibility for this stage of the project. However, it is important to avoid the 'hostage' phenomena which can be associated with placing a user representative in this position. The user can become more of a designer and lose the user perspective which is so important to the design process.

The three important outputs of this phase are the knowledge about the problem, acquired from the expert, the requirements of the end-users, and the knowledge engineers' understanding of the structure of the full system. The demonstrator system itself should be seen as of secondary importance. Indeed it may eventually be discarded altogether. It is paramount to record all the experts' contributions. A rigorous procedure must be adopted, which will ensure that even verbal knowledge contributed over the phone to answer a 'couple of questions' is not lost. Thorough capture, storage and retrieval procedures must be instigated. An initially enthusiastic expert will soon become disaffected if asked to repeat explanations.

The infrastructure developed at this stage of the project will be used throughout the rest of the design.

The other main concern in this phase of the project is the issue of which hardware or software should be used. As we have already outlined, the system has to be flexible. It must respond to feedback from the user. It must be able to provide the user with many options, on an ad-hoc (but recorded) basis.

Also, the restraints which particular hardware and software place on the system should not restrict the user's views and ideas. The best choices at this stage are systems which support very rapid prototyping, multiple methods of input and output and many methods for knowledge representation and inferencing. The system must be capable of providing and demonstrating the many aspects of user interface design, even at the expense of performance.

The current AI market is dominated by Lisp-based toolkits, running on single user workstations, incorporating high resolution displays, WIMPS and flexible software oriented operating systems. Despite the expense of this type of tool, the flexibility and opportunity afforded for development offered by these systems should soon justify their costs. The development of specific systems, such as Trillium, an interface simulator, will provide the designer with a myriad of options.

However, one should not ignore the eventual delivery vehicle and the constraints imposed by external forces. Perhaps a PC oriented system, which could offer some of the features required, will be worth considering. Even in this case, it is recommended that a powerful toolkit is used for prototyping, and that development should only switch to the PC at a later stage.

The main messages of this section have been:

- That the success or failure of the project is likely to hinge on the prototype. It is worth investing in the project at this stage, as the quality of the system will amply justify the cost if the overall project is a success. We believe that up to 20% of the project's overall budget could be spent in getting the prototype right.

- That the expert and the end-users are key figures, who should be fully involved. The organisation running the project must be made aware of the implications of this involvement. This is especially important if the system is being designed to relieve the load on the expert and increase the expert's free time. Indeed, even considering the expensive hardware and software recomended for use in this stage, the most expensive resource will be the expert's time.

10.4.4 System specification

The system should be formally specified. It will contain the detail normally provided in any conventional project. This phase will use information gathered from the previous stages.

However it is not necessary to use the demonstrator, or to build on it.   Often it might be worth discarding the demonstrator in total.   A system which is developed in an evolutionary but piece-meal fashion is likely to lack coherence and consistency, with new ideas thinly painted over the old. However, provided that the system builder has been sufficiently ruthless at the prototyping stage there is no reason why this should necessarily be the case.

The specification will include extensions of the principles formulated during the prototyping.   This information should be a natural output from the prototype, and should be in the form of clearly definable requirements.   The information might be considerably different from that envisaged in the earlier stages of the project, however this also serves as a post-hoc justification of the prototype phase.   For example, it will be possible to incorporate experience gained by actual end-users.

By the time the specification phase has been reached the risk of an unsuccessful project should have been minimised.   The greater than normal risk associated with expert systems should be contained in the prototype phase.   The prototype phase is relatively inexpensive and is the ideal time to assess feasibility and risk.   The specification phase should only be reached it the project is highly likely to succeed.

The approach to expert system building described here should avoid one of the problems with expert systems developments - the problem of failure.   Containing the risks within the prototyping stage means that by the time the full specification is produced, unworkable applications will have been identified with only 10-20% of the budget spent.

The specification should include a complete cost-benefit analysis, and include the significant cost of system 'maturation' (described below) which will be higher than in conventional systems.

One of the problems with this specification is in providing an operational definition of usability.   Shackel (2) describes four main areas.   Before describing these he points out that it is possible to specify and measure usability via operational criteria (described below).   Also, he states that the terms should be given numerical values when the usability goals are set during the design stage of the requirements specifications.

In other words, it is at this stage that the detailed usability requirements must be specified and acted upon.

Usability comprises:

- Effectiveness

    - at better than some required level of performance (eg in terms of speed and errors)

    - by some required percentage of the specified target range of users

    - within some required proportion of the range of usage environments

- Learnability

    - within some specified time from installation and start of user training

    - based upon some specified amount of training and user support

    - within some specified re-learning time each time for intermittent users

- Flexibility

    - with flexibility allowing adaptation to some specified percentage variation in tasks and/or environments beyond those first specified

- Attitude

    - within acceptable levels of human cost in terms of tiredness, discomfort, frustration and personal effort. So that satisfaction causes continued and enhanced usage of the system.

One of the key features of expert system specification in terms of the usability criteria outlined above is flexibility. This is likely to be different from conventional systems.

There is another user issue, which is more applicable to expert systems than to other systems, which is maintainability. A feature of expert systems is that they can be required to be adaptable and maintainable by people other than the designers. The system is able to take new/changed information. Thus a fifth would be in the form of:

● Maintainability

    – an easily updatable knowledge base

There are other issues with system maintainability, which will be covered later.

10.4.5 System implementation

The system implementation will build on th experience gained at the prototyping stage. The knowledge obtained at this stage will be used in the system and the process of knowledge acquisition will continue.

The problems unique to expert systems should be minimised by the time the main system is being produced. For example, the problems of knowledge elicitation, the provision of explanation and the incorporation of user models should be largely solved.

A well designed knowledge representation framework will have been produced and the problems will be in filling in the blanks within the framework and ensuring adequate access to the experts.

The project should be managed using whatever techniques are normally employed by the organisation. This should have emerged during the specification stage, though a human-centred approach is recommended.

Despite this phase representing the stage at which the system is being built, it is one of the least interesting in terms of the problems. The ideal situation is for the implementation to be simple and clear-cut. There should not be problems regarding applicability or whether the system can be built. Provided the previous stages have been followed, we have found that the main expert system problems will have been largely solved.

10.4.6 System evaluation

One of the main problems with expert systems is that the delivery system will not be as complete a system as is normally produced in conventional system design.

Although the performance of the expert system will be lower than it will eventually achieve, it should be at least possible to make a preliminary assessment (see below for some of the reasons). Performance measures might be hard to make if the expert system is not simply replacing an existing role. However, suitable measures should have been specified in the initial studies.

The shortfalls in the expert system as compared to a conventional system will be caused by its knowledge base. A reasonably complex expert system will have an inference engine capable of putting elements of the knowledge base together in an unknown but large number of ways to generate chains of reasoning. Errors will be made, for example where apparently correct knowledge is used out of context, or where knowledge is missing. Scenarios will be encountered which the system builders did not foresee, and the system's performance might be erratic. All these problems will not be encountered until after the system has been passed into regular use. Thus the system's performance may appear much better in an artificial test than, when it is initially used in the field. These problems will be addressed in the next phase.

Despite the incompleteness of the expert system's knowledge base, the HCI interface will essentially be complete and therefore amenable to more rigorous assessment. The system specification will have provided the criteria by which to judge the human factors aspects of the system, although some of the more esoteric aspects might be affected by the underlying knowledge base. For example, an expert system which contained an adaptable interface might not be fully testable until experienced users have evolved. It is not immediately apparent how an adaptable interface should be tested. However, projects such as the Alvey AID project (4) should help define the criteria for a good adaptive interface.

The unique aspects of expert systems can be evaluated only longitudinally i.e. over a fairly long time. For example, use of an expert system may tail off after six months. This might be interpreted in several ways. It might not be the case that the novelty has worn off, but rather that the system has been able to provide users with detailed explanations, training and help that has made them less dependent on it.

Similarly, the system might have the potential for assessing change in policy or the effect of new rules. This is unlikely to be apparent in the early stages of the system's use but will become more obvious as the system develops.

The usual criteria for system evaluation will be appropriate and should have been defined in the specification stage. For example, measures of speed, error rate, mean-time between failure, etc. should be used. Other features, such as the use of training, or an increase in the expert's time available to solve other problems, should also be looked for. It is important to have collected data on peformance of the tasks prior to the introduction of the expert system. This can be then used as the base-line to reassess the performance with the expert system's help. This poses problems associated with the collection of data, eg the natural tendency for performance to improve when looked at closely.

Only if the designer has considered the problems of evaluation before the system has been implemented can accurate evaluation be undertaken.

This is true of both the expert system aspects of the system and for the human-computer interaction.

10.4.7 System maturation

The system delivered will be incomplete. It will have gaps in its knowledge base which will represent areas unforeseen by both the designers and the expert. This state of affairs is somewhat analogous to employing a recently trained technician. Much of the factual knowledge will be in place, as well as some of the practical heuristic knowledge, but there will be problems in the early stages.

The system will need to mature and this will have to be catered for in the early stages of the development cycle. The unique part of an expert system is that the user or expert will be able to add the additional knowledge which the system requires for optimal performance.

This means that the user interface has to be well designed, not only for use, but also for maintenance. Also, the expert system's structure will have to support this function. The interface will also be required to fulfil a training role as well as the conveying of complex information.

The maturation will also involve fairly major modifications. For example, a legislation-based system should be capable of dealing with very significant modifications if the law changes. The changes will also have to be implemented not by the designers but by the end-users and experts. Sometimes these end-users and experts might be different from the ones consulted in the initial design stages.

During the overall design process the users should have become so involved in building the system that they should be capable of making such changes.

10.5 CONCLUSIONS

We have outlined criteria for good system design in building expert systems. This process has emphasised the need to involve the expert and the end-user at all stages. Also, the need for a good user interface has been stressed. This is not only because users are required to use the system but also because they are needed to maintain it.

We have included criteria for the assessment of usability but have not discussed many other aspects of employing human factors in system design. Further information on good, general human factors guidelines can be obtained elsewhere (eg see Singleton (5) and Shackel (6)).

The proposed guidelines emphasise the need for an evolutionary iterative design process, including a comprehensive evaluation. We have also described the need for an evaluation of the task prior to the introduction of the expert system to allow suitable criteria and base-lines to be developed.

The guidelines will increase the likelihood of success. They will minimise the risks commonly associated with the building of expert systems by emphasising the early stages of the process where mistakes are cheap.

The guidelines should provide guidance to the increasing number of people using IKBS techniques to construct novel interfaces to conventional systems, as well as outlining procedures for use throughout any new project.

It is hard to determine how long expert systems will take to construct. In the experience of the authors typical times range from a matter of weeks for an individual to three to four years for a large team.

Much of the justifications for the introduction of expert systems will be in terms of cost-benefit analysis. However, we must develop more accurate techniques for assessing the value of lost knowledge or support of skilled staff.

Expert systems will be more expensive to develop than more conventional systems but it is our assertion that in the long run they will be more economical than non-expert system approaches provided an approach similar to the one outlined here is taken.

The nature of expert systems means that they can be rarely divorced from other issues. The methodology takes little or no account of issues such as the social and economic consequences of introducing expert systems, nor the legal complications which may ensue.

10.6 REFERENCES

1 Parkin A (1980), 'Systems Management' London, Edward Arnold

2 Shackel B (1986), 'Ergonomics in design for Useability' in Proc. 2nd Conf. BCS-HCI Special Interest Group, ed. Harrison and Monk, British Informatics Society Ltd.

3 Coch L and French J R P (1948), 'Overcoming Resistance to Change' Human Relations, 1, pp 511-532

4 The Adaptive Interface Design Project, Alvey Directorate, MMI, Kingsgate House, 66-74 Victoria Street, London SW1E 8SW

5 Singleton W T, Easterby R S and Whitfield D (eds) (1967), 'The Human Operator in Complex Systems' London, Taylor and Francis

6 Shackel B (ed) (1974), 'Applied Ergonomics Handbook' IPC Science and Technology

7. (1985) 'EXPERT SYSTEMS - Some Guidelines', HMSO Information Technology in the Civil Service Series.

Author index

Subject index